OCCASIONS

HOSPITALITY MAKES
FOR INFECTIOUS FUN.

— anonymous

SIMON & SCHUSTER

NEW YORK   LONDON   TORONTO   SYDNEY

always gracious,
sometimes irreverent

OCCASIONS

BY

Kate Spade

edited by Ruth Peltason and Julia Leach

illustrations by Virginia Johnson

HAVE YOU EVER WONDERED...?

Lucky you! You've just inherited your favorite aunt's set of colorful barware.
One problem: which glass is for what drink?

Improvisation and common sense will help you navigate most of the choices. The beauty of an old set of anything is that it allows you to mix it in with your own modern glasses.

It's your first real cocktail party.
What should you have for a well-stocked bar?

A little of this and a little of that are a good beginning: gin, vodka, scotch, whiskey, rum, and tequila are usual requirements as are such additions as Rose's lime juice, tomato juice, tonic, club soda, lemons, and limes.

Giving flowers to a hostess is always a lovely gesture.
Should you send something ahead of time
or bring a bouquet with you?

It might seem old-fashioned or overly formal to you, but sending flowers before a party is the sign of a truly thoughtful guest. It frees up the hostess from last-minute scurrying around just as her guests (and this includes you) are arriving.

You have food allergies, but you dread calling attention to yourself. What do you do when at a sit-down dinner you're served pecan-crusted salmon and you're allergic to nuts?

There are degrees of likely scenarios. If you can scrape off the nuts and still eat the salmon without any worries, do so as gracefully as possible. Otherwise, don't stand on ceremony: let your hostess know, who will no doubt come up with a solution...and one that won't make you sneeze, wheeze, or break out in hives.

You're not a big drinker but your friends are, so at the next cocktail party what's a light drink to request so you won't stand out?

In the summer, try a Virgin Sea Breeze. An all-season favorite is a Virgin Bloody Mary, the spicier the better. And whether you're stateside or in Italy, Campari and soda is a classic choice.

Every time you have dinner at your best friend's, her white tablecloth has a snap and finish to it that makes yours look a bit sad by comparison. How does she keep her whites white, her linens crisp?

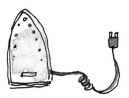

Make sure you only wash whites with whites—no other colors
you a chance to wash with hot water
es. Air-drying outdoors is ideal for
aturally brightening whites, but for most
of us, the gentle cycle in a dryer will have
to do. A good iron, some steam, and a
ttle starch will put some life into your linens.

HAVE YOU EVER WONDERED...?

The hands on the clock are hitting Hour #6 at a cocktail party,
the tarts have long since disappeared, and the candles are stubs.
Out of the corner of your eye, you realize that a lampshade has just
become someone's party hat. Does this mean the party's over?

Sometimes even the plainest "cues" don't work on those guests who have crossed the line from partygoers to party stayers. If people are still enjoying themselves, then do your tired best to keep smiling. But once the décor becomes someone else's wardrobe, by all means call it quits.

How do you balance a drink and an hors d'oeuvre
at a cocktail party without spilling one or dropping the other?

Putting aside those with innate balance, for most of us the act of juggling is an elusive art. It helps to have a small hors d'oeuvre and, better still, to be quick about it. Don't linger and nibble. Eat up! The best hors d'oeuvres are one-bite morsels.

You're determined to give a hostess gift that's not
"the same old thing." But what's special?

How to give something original is the eternal gift-giver's challenge. Don't feel as though you have to invent the wheel each time you select a gift for someone, but do think of that person and his or her interests. Sometimes going to a boutique or even looking in a flea market is a way to find something fresh and unusual.

HAVE YOU EVER WONDERED...?

*You're planning a formal dinner for eight,
but what music will keep the mood light and fun?*

Have on some upbeat music when your
guests are arriving and then "keep the beat"
during the meal as well. Lively music
stimulates conversation and
creates a momentum that lasts
the whole evening long.

*When planning a party, at what point is
mix 'n match more mix than match?
What's the secret to just the "right" balance?*

Planning ahead with a guest list gives you the
time and focus to select among your friends
and acquaintances for any event. It's also a
good idea to plan on a few "backups" in case
of last-minute cancellations. Spontaneous
get-togethers are always fun, but when it comes to a
proper dinner party, sharpen your pencil and start your list.

When is fashionably late just late?

Cocktail parties are forgiving when it comes to
time, though if you arrive after most of the
hors d'oeuvres have disappeared (and half the
guests), then that's a reliable sign you're tardy.
Dinner parties are more time sensitive—if you're
30 minutes past the appointed hour, expect that
your hostess will greet you with an arctic smile.

CONTENTS

Have You Ever Wondered...? **4**

Introduction **10**

SECTION ONE 13

The Mise-en-Scène

Decorating the Room · Shopping for Antiques · Flowers
Lighting · Linens · The Well-Stocked Cupboard
Party Shopping Lists · Music · Seating
When the Out-of-Doors Beckons · Invitations
Dressing the Part · The Good Hostess
The Good Guest · Surprises and Disasters

SECTION TWO 59

Tried 'n True Party Standards

Cocktail Parties · Pre-Party Preparations · Mixed Drinks
Shake, Stir, Pour, and Serve · The Perfect Martini
Champagne and Cognac · Wine is Divine · Beer is a Beverage Too
Hors d'Oeuvres · À la Carte, À Table, and Catering
Dinner Parties · Dinner Party Checklist · Special Dinner Parties
The Art of the Toast · Dinner Party Trivia · Weekend Parties
For the Ideal Guest Room · Weekend Activities in the Country

SECTION THREE 91

An Alphabet of Special Events

Anniversary Gifts · The After-Party Party
Barbecues · Birthdays · Brunches (and Lunches)
Farewell Dinners · Holidays · New Home
Picnics · Showers · Tailgate · Tea
Theme Parties · The Un-Occasion · Weddings

Thank You **108**

Select Bibliography **110**

THE GOOD HOSTESS AND OTHER BRAVE SOULS

"To invite a person to your house is to take charge of his happiness as long as he is beneath your roof."
— *Brillat-Savarin*

I've had the pleasure of being a guest at the homes of so many good hostesses, and I've often wondered what their secret is. Does it mean having a spectacular home for entertaining, being a great cook, knowing the best florists, and surrounding yourself with interesting friends? Or does it mean putting a smile on your face no matter what happens? Actually, I do think the smile is essential and so is humor. Lots of it, as far as I'm concerned. But before the canapés and the soft lighting is one ingredient that I think ultimately defines "the good hostess" and that's grace.

Being gracious when you entertain is perhaps the greatest gift you can give to your guests. It signals acceptance and patience and a go-with-the-flow style that can accommodate spilled wine on the couch (we've had plenty of that!), overcooked lamb chops, and guests who stay well into the witching hour. Graciousness is also about being generous, and the hostesses I most admire are those who make me feel welcomed and relaxed in their homes. The truly generous hostess is one who presses a glass of champagne into my hand and says "Drink up. Enjoy yourself." Making your guests feel at home is truly an art and it's one worth cultivating.

When I was about thirty, I decided it was time to give a proper sit-down dinner. My husband, Andy, was all for it, but he also knew that, considering this would be my first dinner party, a little warning was in order. So he made copies of instructions for the Heimlich maneuver, which he used as the invitation. The point wasn't lost on our friends when Andy wrote, "You're invited to Kate's first dinner party." Hopefully, I've graduated from those early days and by now I've sorted out what I enjoy doing and what's best left to someone else. And that's another point about being a hostess—making sure you surround yourself with people who can help you put on a good party. If you work all day, if you have children, or if you have other primary commitments, then you know that teamwork is essential to anything, and that includes getting ready for a party.

I would never consider myself an expert at being a hostess, but I am a big believer in trying to do my best and looking to others for advice, too. Let's face it: the prospect of giving a cocktail party for thirty or fifty people takes courage and know-how. All my life I've loved books and I often turn to them for inspiration and encouragement. Books are my silent partners in so many things I do. *Occasions* is meant to be a reliable friend, a book I hope you can turn to for ideas and suggestions. Since I love fresh flowers, there's a big section on having flowers at a party (I'm a fan of clear vases and flowers cut short and tightly massed) and another on the sort of music that I think makes people feel happy. You'll find a list of what to stock in your bar for a cocktail party and one filled with ideas for entertaining weekend guests. (Fresh bedding and good reading material are a must. So is private time, for them and you.) The last section of the book is about special occasions. Here you'll find anecdotes about things that Andy and I have enjoyed doing— among our favorites is what Andy calls the Un-Occasion Party, as well as more traditional gatherings such as holidays and tailgate picnics.

Over the years I've learned so much from my family and friends about entertaining, and in so many ways *Occasions* is a tribute to their influence and to all the fun we've shared.

Kate Spade
New York City, 2003

SECTION ONE

The Mise-en-Scène

Decorating the Room · *Shopping for Antiques* · *Flowers*

Lighting · *Linens* · *The Well-Stocked Cupboard*

Party Shopping Lists · *Music* · *Seating*

When the Out-of-Doors Beckons · *Invitations*

Dressing the Part · *The Good Hostess*

The Good Guest · *Surprises and Disasters*

DECORATING THE ROOM

"My husband and I have lived in lots of different places, first out West, and then for nearly twenty years in New York, where 'home' has been a smorgasbord of apartments, each with more than one challenge when it comes to entertaining our friends. My feeling is that you should put your personal stamp on everything—the goal is to reflect your passions. You also need to stay flexible and keep your sense of humor. Entertaining begins with a dream—and then quickly gets overtaken by reality, like the size of your living room! In truth, regardless of the ebb and flow of our homes, there have always been some steady currents along the way."

"I LOVE A PLACE THAT HAS A HINT OF FORMALITY. NOT A LOT, JUST ENOUGH TO MAKE IT SEEM IMPORTANT AND SPECIAL."

SHOPPING FOR YOUR HOME

Antique fairs, flea markets, and the well-chosen design shop are all places to snoop around for things big and small for your home. Sometimes flea markets are where you'll find the less-than-necessary but perfect home accent, such as a pair of Manhattan glass vases or one-of-a-kind serving pieces. Specialty shops are where the owner's careful eye has done some of the legwork of looking for you.

LIGHTING

Imagine walking into a party without any lights. That's how important lighting is. In one quick flick of the switch, lighting establishes the mood in your home. Sconces, chandeliers, floor lamps, or spot lighting will make your guests shine. Indoors or out, candles are an absolute must, both as accent and to softly contour the ambience of your gathering.

FLOWERS

The grace note of every home begins with flowers. The first impression your home makes is less about your furniture than about the sense of beauty and hospitality it conveys. Nothing says "welcome" more than flowers. Cherry blossoms in tall clear vases, anemones lovingly massed, or even a bud vase of lily-of-the-valley in the powder room speak to this kind of gentle beauty.

MUSIC

No celebration is complete without music. Period. Nothing's lonelier than a quiet room at a party, and nothing elevates the spirits like great music (except maybe an equally great cocktail). Make music a priority, and as much a part of your planning as the flowers, table linens, and menu.

LINENS

The wardrobe of any party comes down not to what you're wearing, but how you've dressed your table. Heavy white cotton tablecloths, cocktail napkins in assorted colors and trims, and novelty prints for more festive occasions are key to the look and feel of any event in your home.

THE WELL-STOCKED CUPBOARD

The pantry is the workhorse of your party. Flatware (from sterling silver to French bistro, but never plastic, not even for a picnic), glassware (for everything from orange juice to cocktails and wine), and an arsenal of plates, cups, and special serving pieces are the essentials of entertaining.

SHOPPING FOR ANTIQUES

"One of my favorite things to do is shop flea markets, wherever I am.
It's especially fun when we're vacationing. Sometimes I find a really great
old china pattern that I know will perfectly complement our silver at home.
It comes down to trying to balance new and old."

Looking for a picnic table? Need some lamps for your guest room, linens
for parties, or fun highball glasses for the Fourth of July? Flea markets
are wide-open treasure chests of *stuff*, some of it pricey, most of it
affordable. And the best part? No one else will have the same thing.

ITEMS TO SHOP FOR AT THE FLEA MARKET

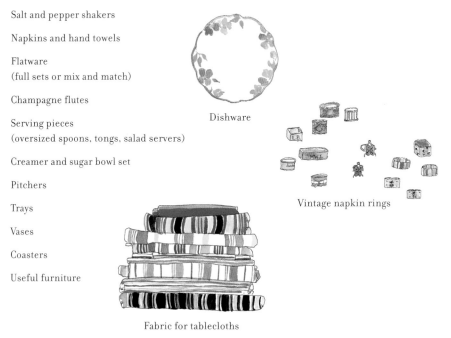

Salt and pepper shakers

Napkins and hand towels

Flatware
(full sets or mix and match)

Champagne flutes

Serving pieces
(oversized spoons, tongs, salad servers)

Creamer and sugar bowl set

Pitchers

Trays

Vases

Coasters

Useful furniture

Dishware

Vintage napkin rings

Fabric for tablecloths

WHERE TO SHOP

Brimfield Antiques Show
Brimfield, Mass.

Various antique shops
Hudson, N.Y.

Stormville Airport
Flea Market
Stormville, N.Y.

John Derian Company
New York City

Steven Sclaroff
New York City

Alan Moss Studio
New York City

Sag Street Antiques
Sag Harbor, N.Y.

Farmington Antique
Weekends
Farmington, Conn.

Scott Antique Market
Atlanta, Ga.

Kane County Fair
St. Charles, Ill.

Architectural Artifacts
Chicago

Rose Bowl Flea Market
Pasadena, Calif.

West Palm Beach Antique and
Collectibles Show
West Palm Beach, Fla.

Lincoln Road Antique Market
Miami Beach, Fla.

Paris Flea Market (also
known as Marché aux Puces,
Porte de Clignancourt,
St. Ouen)
Paris

Burmondsey Market
London

Christopher Gibb
London

New Caledonian Market
London

HANDY SHOPPING TIPS

Negotiating is part of the game. Have plenty of cash on hand.
("I'm terrible at it, so I ask someone else to help me.")

Blend in: here's one time where you do want to look like
everyone else. No fancy jewelry, spiffy outfits. Casual is cool.

It's okay to be a snoop. Look. Dig. Then dig again. (Maybe a big old stuffed animal is covering
up silver napkin rings.)

If you must have it, then don't hesitate. (Or else be prepared to have some other shopper
swoop down and buy what you love.)

Consider how to get your purchase home *before* you commit.

And remember: the early bird gets the worm (or the table!).

FLOWERS

"As far as I'm concerned, the best thing about an indoor party is cut flowers. In fact, I can't imagine my life without having flowers around, and a party is just another reason to have them for everyone to enjoy. I try not to think about my budget first, and concentrate instead on the effect I want, the colors I have in mind. Then I look at my wallet."

"ONCE THERE WAS A MAN NAMED MR. POWERS,
HE WAS LONELY BECAUSE HIS WIFE FIXED FLOWERS..."

—OGDEN NASH, "THE SOLITUDE OF MR. POWERS"

Flowers will reward you with longer blooms if you change the water daily and diagonally cut 1 to 2 inches off the ends.

ABOUT ARRANGEMENTS

"For me, flowers should never be pretentious and lord their beauty over everything else around them. I like to pay attention to my flowers, but I don't care for all the fuss. So I'm not really an 'arrangements girl' (and I guess I'm not really a 'stem girl,' either). I like my flowers trimmed pretty close to the flower itself, and I like to see them tightly massed in short bowls—glass or crystal are my usual candidates. When I can't be bothered with all the trimming of stems and cleaning of vases, I'll take an armful of fresh flowers and plunk them into a nice china pitcher for the table. And I do my best to make any stray tendrils look deliberate."

I REALLY LOVE...

Peonies, my absolute
favorite, especially coral

Sweet peas

Hydrangea—cut short and
tightly packed so they
resemble snowballs

Lisianthus
(preferably white)

Anemones

Ranunculus

Poppies

Dahlias, the more petals
the better

Cherry blossoms—
deep pink and very tall

Flowering quince

Cattails

Roses—big, fat,
and best used as a
stand-in for peonies

French tulips (but no
ruffled petals, please)

Orange trees

TRIMMING THE ORANGE TREE

Hang ornaments or string little sparkly lights
from a potted orange tree. (For special occasions,
you can rent the tree from your local nursery.)

IN PRAISE OF PEONIES

Peonies were "employed in the choicest room and table decorations, as bouquets for drawing rooms and smart weddings—in fact, their presence is welcomed everywhere," remarked the women's magazine *Fashions and Fancies* in 1899. It's still true.

MY WISH LIST OF FLOWERS, MONTH BY MONTH

JANUARY
Tulips, ranunculus, anemones, forsythia, magnolia branches

FEBRUARY
Tulips, hydrangeas, ranunculus, poppies, anemones, forsythia, nerine, flowering quince

MARCH
Peonies, tulips, hydrangeas, ranunculus, anemones, dogwood, nerine, freesia, flowering crabapple, cherry blossoms

APRIL
Peonies, tulips, hydrangeas, ranunculus, anemones, nerine, freesia, flowering dogwood, cherry blossoms

MAY
Peonies, tulips, ranunculus, hydrangeas, lily-of-the-valley, anemones, freesia, flowering dogwood

JUNE
Peonies, tulips, lilacs, hydrangeas, dahlias, poppies

JULY
Hydrangeas, sweet pea, dahlias, lisianthus, eucalyptus

AUGUST
Hydrangeas, dahlias, cosmos, black-eyed Susans, eucalyptus

SEPTEMBER
Dahlias, cosmos, hydrangeas

OCTOBER
Hydrangeas, cosmos, freesia, maple leaves

NOVEMBER
Ranunculus, peonies, anemones, freesia

DECEMBER
Tulips, ilex berries, freesia

"Although I'm always saying how much I like cut flowers in clear glass vases, frankly there are plenty of times when I reach for something else. But that 'something else' always has to be simple. Fussy vases crowd the natural beauty of flowers."

FLORAL AROMATICS FOR THE BEDROOM AND BATH...

Freesia

Honeysuckle

Jasmine

Lilacs

Lily-of-the-valley

Paperwhites

Sweet pea

Tuberose

Gardenias

The ends of flowering branches and shrubs should be (gently) smashed with a hammer to help the water travel up the stem. Or you can use a sharp paring knife to score vertical lines along the bottom of the stem.

Empress Josephine Bonaparte (1763–1814) added peonies to her gardens at Malmaison. She also had a gown decorated with orange silk peony petals.

LIGHTING

"When it comes to scented candles, I find it calming to keep one burning in my office, I like to use them in the powder room, and when I travel, I always put some in my hotel room, no matter where I stay. Somehow the fragrance gives a little more personality and familiarity to the room. For entertaining, though, I think white votives are simple and pretty, so I scatter them randomly around the room—on windowsills, along a stairway, or lining a ledge of some sort.

Votives create a hush, and make people feel they can share their innermost thoughts, or just have a good laugh together. The idea is to let the votives set a mood for good conversation."

"I'VE NEVER MET A MOISTURE CREAM THAT COULD IMPROVE ON THE GLOW OF SOFT LIGHTING."

Carpe diem! Gathering special candles as you come across them on your journeys will come in handy when you entertain. (You'll also find that they make perfect gifts when you're the guest at a summer dinner on the terrace.)

In most homes, a dimmer will allow you to set the mood—and radiance of your guests—with just a simple flick of the wrist.

EATING OUTDOORS?

Try lighting your table from the ground up, literally. Arrange votives on the lawn so that they form a wide (and magical) ring around your table. Set more votives on the table itself. Everyone will glow.

CRYSTAL CHANDELIERS
ARE THE GRANDES
DAMES OF LIGHTING.

LIGHTS I LIKE...

"Overhead fixtures are first about function, and
always about form. My favorite fixtures at home
are antique crystal, especially when they're
turned down low at a special dinner and send
light in 1,000 directions. Low lighting is the
color of champagne, and sheds a shimmery beauty
around a room. For contrast, I think a big chandelier—
really overscaled with swags of crystal pendants—is all
about making elegant statements."

TALL OR SHORT
BUT ALWAYS THIN...

"The designer Ted Muehling makes
candles in different heights, and all
of them are very thin. I like to put
them on the dining table and spread
them all so that they're just barely
longer than normal candelabra.
To me, it's more modern this way.
Plus, it looks so easy and because
they are so thin you can easily see
between them. There's a little
bounce to a room with all that
flickering light. I find that a dining
room table without candles is flat."

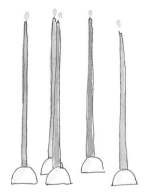

TRY TALL PINK CANDLES
ON YOUR PICNIC TABLE.

A lighted candle in the
window—known as a
welcome candle—is a
sign of hospitality.

LINENS

"I must say that I would choose cloth napkins over paper any day of the week, and for just about any occasion. I love love *love* cocktail napkins embroidered with bugs—my favorite is a black spider, though I can see why some people might find that a bit off-putting. When it comes to a sit-down dinner, though, I stick with the classics and go with a strong white linen napkin. Why not? It always looks great and it's easy to have a healthy collection of them without spending much money. I do think a paper cocktail napkin printed for a special occasion is smart, but then again I would want the message to be in a bright color."

BEFORE YOU SET OUT TO BUY A THING...

first consider what you already have on hand.

TABLE LINENS
Tablecloths, place mats, napkins, cocktail napkins

BEDDING
Sheets, pillowcases, duvet covers, extra blankets for chilly nights

BATH
Bath sheets, bath towels, hand towels, washcloths, and fluffy robes and slippers for special overnight guests

COUNT AND SORT YOUR NAPKINS
If you have a specific pattern or color, eight is ideal, and six works too. If you want to have a lot of the same napkin, see what you can find at a flea market. Sometimes the best values are those you discover when you're traveling.

NO CREASES ALLOWED
Table napkins are best ironed flat, then folded and smoothed by hand. If you want to store them flat, wrap them around old gift-wrap tubes. When it's time to use them, they'll be like soft meringues.

GETTING THE HANG OF IT

For a dinner, a tablecloth should hang over the edge eight to twelve inches.

MEASUREMENTS

Luncheon napkins:
12 x 12" to 18 x 18"

Cocktail napkins:
even smaller than above

Dinner napkins:
18 x 18" to 24 x 24"

Banquet napkins:
24 x 24" to 32 x 32"

SIMPLE IS SUBLIME

"Although I subscribe to simple is sublime, napkin rings can be great as another accessory for the table. I like mine on the humorous side (overscaled or tiny tiny, and always inexpensive).
I love ribbon, so sometimes I'll make soft bows with striped grosgrain."

Buy a white tablecloth. Have it embroidered with the names of your favorite foods or travel destinations.

"MUCH AS I LOVE STRONG COLOR, I LIKE MY TABLECLOTHS WHITE AND SOFTLY IRONED. OCCASIONALLY, I'LL THROW ON SOMETHING WITH A REALLY GREAT PATTERN. WHITE CHINA AGAINST A PATTERN IS A WELCOME RELIEF."

FOR THE GUEST ROOM

Matching set of towels (and in good condition, please)

Freshly ironed white sheets with a hint of trim

American quilts, deeply colored (and that includes pink)

Shams and comforters, with patterns and bold colors

FOR THE TABLE, HOW ABOUT...

Fabrics you've picked up while traveling

An assortment of your great-aunt's 1950s tablecloths and matching napkins

Reliable, plain white linen

Cotton fabric from the neighborhood fabric store (cut the edges with pinking shears)

HANDY WITH AN IRON

For a perfectly ironed tablecloth, first dampen the cotton with a sprinkling of warm water on one side (linen needs to be even more damp). Round tablecloths should be ironed from the center out toward the edges, turning the cloth as you go. For square or rectangular cloths, fold them in half lengthwise, iron on the wrong side until partially dry, reverse, and iron the right side. Refold and repeat for the other half.

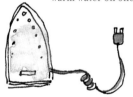

ODE TO THE IRONED SHEET

Just as showers have come to replace long soaks in the tub, most of us settle for freshly laundered sheets rather than laundered *and ironed*. But if you can find the time, indulge yourself and your guests by taking up this near-forgotten art. Sleeping on ironed sheets is heavenly. All-cotton sheets take some effort to iron well, and are helped by spritzing with a little water and using the steam setting. Some people like to iron their sheets while still damp, which also means less stress on the sheet in the dryer. Of course, you always have the option to iron just the pillowcases. (Premium indulgence is sending out your sheets to be ironed. But be prepared to pay for this special service.)

BEDS AND BED LINENS

Although there are some variations in mattress and sheet sizes, custom still dictates standard sizes (unless you are buying European sheets).

MATTRESSES

Twin (or single): 39 x 75"

Full (or double): 54 x 75"

Queen: 60 x 80"

King: 78 x 80"

California King: 72 x 84"

BED SHEETS

Twin flat: 66 x 96"

Twin fitted: 39 x 75"

Full (or double) flat: 81 x 96"

Full fitted: 54 x 75"

Queen flat: 90 x 102"

Queen fitted: 60 x 80"

King flat: 108 x 102"

King fitted: 78 x 80"

California king flat: 102 x 110"

California king fitted: 72 x 84"

(p.s. If you have an extra-thick mattress, you may need a larger flat sheet, so measure the depth of the mattress before investing in new sheets. Some flat sheets come in an extra-long length for just this reason.)

PILLOWCASES

Standard: 20 x 26"

Queen: 20 x 30"

King: 20 x 40"

European: 26 x 26"

Boudoir: 12 x 16"

Neck roll: 6 x 14"

WELCOME THE COMFORTER

More and more, Americans have been won over by down comforters whereas thirty years ago the electric blanket was more widely in use. And that has meant another bedding consideration: the duvet cover.

Twin: 68 x 88"; 68 x 86"; 66 x 88"

Full: 81 x 88"

Full/queen: 86 x 86"; 88 x 88"

King: 107 x 96"; 102 x 86"; 102 x 88"

THE WELL-STOCKED CUPBOARD
FLATWARE, GLASSWARE, PLATES, CUPS, AND OTHER TABLE SUNDRIES

"Use what you have. If you don't have sterling silver, then you probably won't need it. If your taste runs to modern, then I say, lean into it, expand on that approach. With few exceptions, the traditional dinner party composed strictly of sterling silver and crystal is no longer something any of us have to worry about. In fact, that's my point: 'strict' doesn't belong in our vocabulary any more when it comes to setting the table."

KNOW YOUR SILVER

STERLING SILVER
Comes in three weights (light, medium, and heavy) and by law is stamped "sterling" on the back. Sterling silver is elegance personified and its durability ensures it will last more than one lifetime. Often monogrammed.

"STERLING SILVER IS UNDENIABLY MORE ELEGANT THAN SILVER PLATE OR STAINLESS STEEL....THE MOST IMPORTANT CONSIDERATION IS WEIGHT, FOR IT IS VERY DISAGREEABLE TO EAT WITH FEATHERWEIGHT UTENSILS, AND YOU SHOULD ALWAYS TRY TO SELECT KNIVES AND FORKS THAT FEEL SLIGHTLY HEAVY IN THE HAND."

—GENEVIÈVE ANTOINE DARIAUX

"WHETHER YOU PLAN TO BUY PLATED OR STERLING SILVER, PLAIN SILVER IN A SIMPLE SHAPE IS USUALLY THE WISEST CHOICE."

—VOGUE'S BOOK OF ETIQUETTE

SILVER PLATE

Flatware whose silver has been plated onto a base metal. The heavier the plate, the more durable and usually the more costly. Takes well to polishing.

STAINLESS STEEL

Modern, inexpensive, long-lasting, and easy to care for. Most flatware designed today is stainless steel. Unlike sterling silver and silver plate, stainless steel never needs polishing.

COUNTING, MATCHING, AND MIXING

Most of us have stockpiled things over the years, and it's not until we have a party that we "unearth" what we so carefully stowed away. Open your cupboards, bring down your boxes, and start counting. Practice a few mix and match combinations before your actual dinner party.

FLATWARE

"Over the years, the rules governing flatware and its uses have changed considerably. More than seventy-five years ago, a formally set table would have as many as sixteen pieces of silver per person. Mercifully, today's dinner party uses half that. One piece of advice that I've found helpful remains the same: the traditional 'service for twelve' gives you the greatest flexibility."

THE DINING TABLE TODAY

FORKS
table fork, salad fork

KNIVES
table knife, dessert knife

SPOONS
soup spoon, dessert or after-dinner spoon

SILVERWARE I'D LIKE TO SEE ON
THE 21st-CENTURY TABLE
The noble dessert fork,
a happy hybrid of a fork and spoon.
Ideal for strawberry-rhubarb pie à la mode,
chocolate mousse, or peach cobbler.

ONCE USED, UTENSILS SHOULD NEVER TOUCH THE TABLE LINENS,
BUT REST GRACEFULLY ON THE EDGE OF A PLATE OR SAUCER.

DON'T WORRY ABOUT BEING "MATCHY-MATCHY." ESTATE SALES
ARE GREAT PLACES TO FIND CLEVER ADDITIONS TO YOUR SILVER.

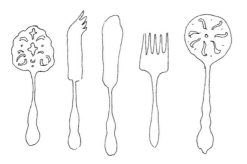

Flatware for this and that: tomato server, cheese knife,
butter knife, sardine fork, large tomato server

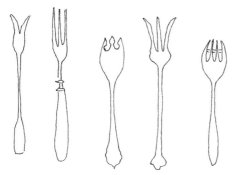

Fork heaven: oyster fork, fruit fork, dessert or
ice cream fork, lettuce fork, ramekin fork

"S" IS FOR SHINE

Before a party, recount your
silver and polish any that
has become tarnished.

To keep sterling silver
its shiniest, use it. Like
buffing your nails, too
much polishing takes off
the top layer, including
the monogram.

Polish sterling silver with
good-quality silver polish.
Rinse well and dry thoroughly
with a soft linen cloth. Air
drying can result in spotting.

HOTEL SILVER

Quality, durability, and affordability are a tricky threesome. That's
where hotel silver comes in, the hotelier's solution for the dining
table. The best is heavily plated and sometimes bears the crest or
name of the hotel. In all fairness, hotel silver was also traditionally
used aboard ocean liners, trains, and until recently, on airplanes.
It has become a collectible today, no doubt for the souvenir aspect
of the stamped insignias.

WHEN OLDER IS BETTER...

Do you have some odd forks, knives, and spoons in the sterling silver you inherited? You can still use them, and probably in ways our grandparents never imagined.

Spear a cerignola olive with a butter pick.

Flat tomato servers are perfect for lifting pancakes (unless they're giant flapjacks).

An old-fashioned cheese scoop is a fun way to serve fresh cantaloupe and blueberries.

A gravy ladle makes serving little roly-poly peas easier.

Tiny salt spoons can be used to serve spicy sauces.

Use a demitasse spoon to scoop out the marrow in osso buco.

The traditional tablespoon can double as a serving spoon or as a cradle for twirling long strands of linguini.

DINNERWARE

Like flatware, the best dishes combine beauty and usefulness. The beauty of everyday china—often purchased in an open-stock pattern—is that it can be used over and over again, and can be readily replaced. The beauty of fine china is exactly that—it's beautiful. And much more costly to replace. (If you purchase fine china abroad, the replacement value soars.)

A place setting for everyday is pretty basic—dinner plate, maybe a salad plate—but when it comes to setting the table for a dinner party, there are more choices . . . and usually more china. Whatever style you purchase, consider how many your table seats, how easy it is (or isn't) to replace broken or chipped pieces, and your budget. A place setting for eight is perhaps the minimum, and if you entertain frequently—and you have a large table—then twelve place settings are right for you.

YOU NEVER KNOW . . .

Dinnerware basics are a must-have, but keep your eye out for the oddball-sized dishes. The unexpected salad plate or bowl shows style and imagination.

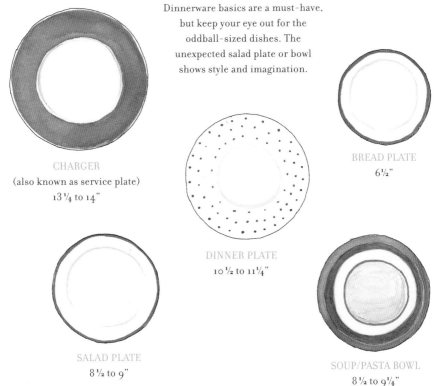

CHARGER
(also known as service plate)
13 ¼ to 14"

BREAD PLATE
6½"

DINNER PLATE
10 ½ to 11¼"

SALAD PLATE
8 ½ to 9"

SOUP/PASTA BOWL
8 ½ to 9¼"

GLASSWARE FOR THE HOME BAR

Of the many objects used for home entertaining,
glassware is among the most traditional.

GLASS	DESCRIPTION	USES
BEER GLASSES	I like the pilsner, with its deep shaft and statuesque proportions. 10–14 ounces	Keep with tradition and use the pilsner only for beer. Beer mugs, however, can also be used for iced coffee, ice-cream sodas, or root beer floats.
BRANDY SNIFTERS	More about shape than size, where trapping the aroma in the bowl is instant Zen. 4–24 ounces	Dare to be different. At your next formal luncheon use brandy snifters for apple cider (in the fall) or lemonade (in high summer).
CHAMPAGNE GLASSES	The flute still makes the loveliest music, but when you sip from the wide glass bowl, you'll feel like you're in an old Hollywood movie. 6–10 ounces	A single-berry concoction is a perfect mate with a champagne glass. Raspberries are lovely, and mango looks especially delicious if you use a melon-ball scoop.
COLLINS GLASSES	Thinner than a highball. 10–14 ounces	A natural for a Tom or Rum Collins.
CORDIALS	Very small, also known as "ponies."	Fill with wood matches and keep on the side of the bar.

GLASS	DESCRIPTION	USES
HIGHBALL GLASSES	Ice + liquor + mixer. The basic of any barware, here or abroad. 8–12 ounces	Accommodates everything from Gin and Tonics to Bloody Marys, even beer.
JUICE GLASSES	Small, often inexpensive, and can vary widely in design.	Juice, of course! Great also for casual servings of chianti.
MARTINI GLASSES	Perfect.	Nowadays a martini glass is filled with everything but grape-nuts. But why mess with a classic? Only a martini belongs in a martini glass.
OLD-FASHIONED GLASSES	Want your scotch on the rocks? Then this is the glass for you. 4–10 ounces	It's summer, so enjoy a Half-and-Half in this glass— ½ lemonade and ½ iced tea.
SHOT GLASSES	This one-sip-only glass is not just for pouring and measuring. 2 ounces	Here's how you serve your best whiskey neat, your tequila fast.
WINEGLASSES	For good reason, red wine is best in a balloon-shaped glass, white wine in a smaller glass, typically with a narrower nose. Red wine: 8–14 ounces White wine: 6–8 ounces	Non-drinkers appreciate bubbly water in a wineglass with a fruit slice.

PARTY SHOPPING LISTS

"Parties can be as simple and as casual as you want them to be. And that goes for your party food as well. Sometimes the season determines the type of party you're giving, or the location. In my opinion, ease and practicality begin with being organized."

MEXICAN COCKTAIL PARTY

It seems just about everybody loves guacamole, with its velvety bite and aromatic cilantro. Icy cold beer is a great chaser, but if tequila is your preference, by all means make up fresh batches of margaritas.

- ☐ Avocadoes, very ripe
- ☐ Red onion
- ☐ Fresh cilantro
- ☐ Limes
- ☐ Kosher or chunky sea salt
- ☐ Tortilla chips
- ☐ Salsa—2 or 3 flavors, such as tomato, green chile, and mango
- ☐ Pacifico beer
- ☐ Designated driver

MUSIC

- ☐ *Y Tu Mamá También* soundtrack
- ☐ *Teatro*, Willie Nelson
- ☐ *Jugo a La Vida*, Los Tucanes de Tijuana
- ☐ Live mariachi band

GUACAMOLE—TRADITIONAL AND MODERN

For a TRADITIONAL GUACAMOLE, slice and pit the avocadoes. Roughly mash, and stir in finely chopped red onion and fresh lime juice. Season to taste with salt.

FRUITY AND FIERY GUACAMOLE: Follow the instructions above. Add chopped ripe pear, halved red grapes, pomegranate seeds, and minced fresh serrano chiles.

CHUNKY AND SPICY GUACAMOLE: Prepare the traditional guacamole, and add chopped radishes and jalapeño peppers.

BONFIRE AT THE BEACH

In our lexicon, the ideal definition of an outdoor party is one without walls. (And perfect for non-cooks too.) Be sure to round up some twigs for roasting marshmallows.

- [ ] Hot dogs
- [ ] Hamburgers
- [ ] Buns for each
- [ ] Cheese—American and Monterey Jack with peppers
- [ ] Mustard—ballpark and Dijon
- [ ] Ketchup
- [ ] Corn on the cob
- [ ] Dill pickles
- [ ] Potato chips
- [ ] Marshmallows
- [ ] Blueberry pie
- [ ] Neon frisbees
- [ ] A sunny disposition

MUSIC

- [ ] *Pet Sounds*, The Beach Boys
- [ ] *Sunshine Hit Me*, A Band of Bees
- [ ] *Invincible Summer*, k.d. lang
- [ ] Laughter, waves, seagulls

GRILLED CORN ON THE COB THREE WAYS

SIMPLE CORN: Keep the stem intact. Pull down the husks and remove the silk. Soak for 15 minutes in cold water. Twist husks at ends and grill the corn over medium heat until nicely charred and cooked through, about 15 minutes. Turn from time to time.

HERB CORN: Follow the method above, but before twisting together the husks, add pats of good butter and sprinkle on some chopped fresh dill.

SOUTH-OF-THE-BORDER CORN: Remove the silk. In a bowl, combine shredded cotija cheese, butter, and cayenne pepper. Spread it on the corn, pull up the husks, and grill, turning from time to time. Have plenty of napkins on hand.

JAPANESE SPRING DINNER FOR SIX

Fresh sushi and sashimi, edamame, cold sake . . . what could be better? Answer: why, having it delivered, of course! Invite like-minded sushi lovers, and order in a variety of appetizers, sushi, and green tea ice cream for dessert. Brightly colored chopsticks are a festive addition to the table. Serve the ice cream in celadon teacups.

- ☐ Gyoza (steamed Japanese dumplings)
- ☐ Oshitashi (cold spinach)
- ☐ Hijiki (cold seaweed salad)
- ☐ Edamame
- ☐ Green salad
- ☐ Yellowtail and scallion roll
- ☐ Shrimp and cucumber roll
- ☐ Spicy tuna roll
- ☐ Spider roll (with soft shell crab)
- ☐ Godzilla roll
- ☐ Dragon roll
- ☐ Soy sauce
- ☐ Fresh wasabi and pickled ginger
- ☐ Sake
- ☐ Kirin, Sapporo, and Asahi beers
- ☐ Green tea ice cream

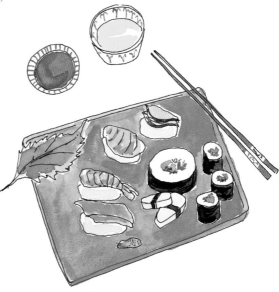

MUSIC

- ☐ *Made in U.S.A.*, Pizzacato Five
- ☐ *Lennon Legend*, John Lennon
- ☐ *Beauty*, Ryuichi Sakamoto
- ☐ *Yoshimi Battles the Pink Robots*, The Flaming Lips

HOW TO PICK UP YOUR STICKS

Pick up a chopstick in the middle, as you would a pencil; then hold it between your thumb and index finger, with support from your third and fourth fingers. The second chopstick should be parallel to the first, secured between your thumb and index finger.

MIDNIGHT BREAKFAST FOR TWO

You've been dancing, it's late, and you're famished. What better time to make something quick, but with a dash of elegance, such as a plate of softly scrambled eggs with salmon caviar. Even easier would be toast with butter and jam, washed down with cold beer.

- ☐ 6 eggs
- ☐ 1 oz salmon caviar, domestic
- ☐ Fresh bread, crusts removed
- ☐ Unsalted butter
- ☐ Chilled Pouilly-Fuissé

MUSIC

- ☐ *Moonlight Serenade*, Glenn Miller and his orchestra
- ☐ *Puttin' on the Ritz*, Fred Astaire
- ☐ *So Tonight That I Might See*, Mazzy Star
- ☐ *Midnite Vultures*, Beck (if you still feel like dancing)

SCRAMBLED EGGS WITH SALMON CAVIAR

In a medium bowl beat the eggs with a couple tablespoons of water or milk and some fresh pepper. Melt two tablespoons of butter in a sauté pan, and when bubbling stir in the eggs. Cook slowly over low heat, gently forming the eggs into soft curds. Once they begin to set, immediately remove them from the heat (they will continue to cook a bit more) and divide them among two of your best china plates. Top each serving with a generous dollop of caviar, and enjoy with hot buttered toast. An accompanying glass of chilled wine is a must.

MUSIC

"The right mix of guests, great food, abundant flowers, and sparkling candles are all essential to pulling off a memorable party. Yet, for me, if the music isn't well thought-out—upbeat, catchy songs—well, I wouldn't say the party's a bust, but it's more than a few shades shy of perfect. I almost always prefer that the music be lively, even during dinner. Keep the momentum going and the volume up, but with consideration for your guests' conversation. Don't put on more dance songs if you're trying to gently shoo your friends out the door. But I find anything too mellow slows down the momentum of the party."

FAVORITE PARTY SONG MIX

"Heavy Metal Drummer," Wilco

"You Belong to Me," Elvis Costello

"Up with People," Lambchop

"Best of My Love," The Emotions

"One by One All Day," The Shins

"Oh La La," The Faces

"Beautiful Head," The National

"Polythene Pam," The Beatles

"She Came in Through the Bathroom Window,"
 The Beatles

"Cecilia," Simon & Garfunkel

"Sound & Vision," The Sea and Cake

"Fill Your Heart," David Bowie

"Rhythm King," Luna

"Takin' It to the Streets," Doobie Brothers

"Friendly Ghost," Eels

"Oh Yoko," John Lennon

"She," The Sundays

"Madeline," Yo La Tengo

"The Politics of Sway," Chris Lee

"Water No Get Enemy," D'Angelo, Femi Kuti,
 Macy Gray and The Soultronics (featuring Nile
 Rodgers and Roy Hargrove)

"Message of Love," Pretenders

"Big Yellow Taxi," Joni Mitchell

"Lazy Flies," Beck

"You're My Best Friend," Queen

"Don't Stop," Fleetwood Mac

SUGGESTED MUSIC FOR...

MAY DAY SUNDAY BRUNCH

Sympathique, Pink Martini

This is...Beaumont, Beaumont

Romantica, Luna

The Best of Bill Evans on Verve, Bill Evans

Nancy Wilson & Cannonball Adderly, Nancy Wilson and Cannonball Adderly

GIRLS' POKER NIGHT

Exile on Main St., The Rolling Stones

Fever In Fever Out, Luscious Jackson

Houses of The Holy, Led Zeppelin

Blues, Nina Simone

Car Wheels on a Gravel Road, Lucinda Williams

BASTILLE DAY FÊTE

CQ, motion picture soundtrack

Comic Strip, Serge Gainsbourg

The 'Yeh-Yeh' Girl from Paris, Françoise Hardy

Miss Kitt to You, Eartha Kitt

Amélie, motion picture soundtrack

"I'm a convert to the multi-CD changer. When I'm getting ready for a party, I choose five CDs, hit 'play' just as the first guest rings the bell and then I don't worry about the music until I have to hit 'stop' at the end of the night (or afternoon, as the case may be). Best to put some thought into which CD plays first—set the tone, get people's toes tapping—and which goes last. As much as I like to keep things festive, I tend to wind things down with a more laid-back selection."

SEATING

"When it comes to seating, I want to make sure that everyone has a good time, and I don't want the arrangement of people too predictable, so I try not to put too many people together who know one another. As for couples, I like to break them up, but I think it depends on the couple. I'm not religious about it. For instance, if the couple has never been to my home before, or if they're newlyweds, or maybe just a little nervous or insecure, then I put them beside or across from each other."

FROM WHERE I SIT...

"I like to sit at the top or head of the table. This way I have an aerial view of the party and I can keep tabs to make sure that everyone is in conversation with some-one, or whether someone needs a glass of wine. If Andy is at one end and I'm at the other, it puts parameters on the table and everyone tends to feel included."

"THE HEAD OF THE TABLE IS WHEREVER THE HOSTESS SITS."

—EMILY POST

PLACE CARDS

"We like to use place cards at our parties.
Sometimes we use little holders, but usually
we set them flat on the table, above the plate.
Instead of paper, we've had cookies made
and inscribed with the names of our guests."

"Whenever there are single people at a sit-down dinner, of
course I seat them beside their date or chaperone. But if
they don't arrive with a date or special person, then I place
them next to someone I think they'd feel comfortable with.
Or beside someone new that they might want to know."

As a guest, before you even think of switching around the place cards,
remember that a good guest is also a good sport: sit where you're seated.

Seating your guests is harder than checkers, easier than chess. Like the players on a board, each person has his or her own persona, and that's where the fun comes in. Your job: keep the conversation going and the wine flowing.

THE MALE PERSPECTIVE

"If there is a guy who's kind of shy and doesn't talk easily, then we like to put him beside a cute girl who likes to flirt. It always works. It gets the guy out of his shell, and it seems to make the girl pretty happy too."

—Andy Spade

BALANCING THE FUN

"When there's more than one table, my first thought is how to place everyone so that each table is fun. In that case, I spread out the vivacious people, and try to have at least one really spirited person at a table. The last thing I want is for a guest to be looking at some other table thinking, 'I want to be over there, at *that* table.'"

A GOOD RULE OF THUMB IS TO ESTIMATE TWENTY-FOUR INCHES PER PERSON AT THE TABLE

ADJECTIVES ARE A BEAUTIFUL THING...

No matter how often she entertains, a hostess always faces the same challenge: how to create a fresh and lively atmosphere. One way is to put a spin on the traditional seating card. Who needs place cards with proper names when a well-aimed adjective will do? Write out cards with *coy, funny, nosey, flirtatious, bachelor, cunning,* and *quiet.* Let your guests select their own places at the table.

WHEN THE OUT-OF-DOORS BECKONS

"If you have enough indoor space for entertaining, then you can confidently give parties at home year-round. But when considerations of space become challenging, which is true for most of us, then to the outdoors you must go. Aside from mosquitoes and other night creatures (which you need to plan for), entertaining alfresco is a luxury available to all. It's also a way to have a more casual and spontaneous get-together."

OUTDOOR DINING MEANS...

Japanese hanging lanterns

Lazy dips in the pool

No fear of getting sunburned

Picnic tables covered in white cloth and decorated with flowers from your garden

Badminton between courses

Dressing casually

Masses of votives

Not worrying about spills on carpets and couches

Bamboo torches
(good for beating back bugs, too)

Midnight lawn tennis with glow-in-the-dark tennis balls

Throwing open the French doors and moving the inside outside

"I LOVE COLORFUL PAPER LANTERNS FOR DINING ALFRESCO. I'VE FOUND THEM IN THE MARKETS OF HONG KONG, AND IN MY ADOPTED CITY, NEW YORK."

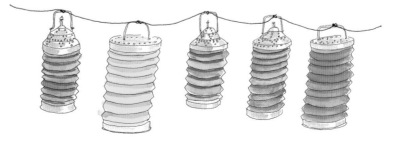

INVITATIONS

"To me, there's no such thing as *the* perfect invitation, because I love so many kinds. But I'm pretty consistent about a couple of things: nothing is better than fine letterpress printing and witty copy. I like information, and I especially like to think of something that will make someone smile or chuckle a little. Again, it's all about balance and avoiding anything that takes itself too seriously."

SAVE THE DATE

Certain times of year the calendar can become clogged with events, such as around Christmastime or the Fourth of July. As a way of securing your guests' availability, you can send out a postcard four to six weeks in advance with a little note about "saving the date." People appreciate the thoughtful gesture. Follow up with the actual invitation about two weeks before your party.

THE ESSENTIAL INVITE CONTAINS...

It probably seems obvious what to include in your invitation, but don't be fooled—sometimes the most basic things get overlooked.

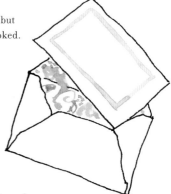

WHAT THE EVENT IS

WHEN

WHERE

TIME AND DATE

WHO'S GIVING THE PARTY

RSVP

Whether there is a SPECIAL OCCASION or reason for the party and whether your guests need to bring something (especially if it's a birthday party or baby shower)

A PERSONAL NOTE is optional as is indicating style of dress

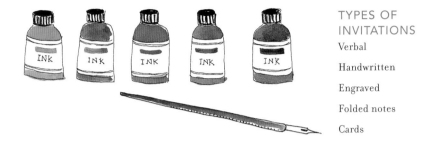

TYPES OF INVITATIONS

Verbal

Handwritten

Engraved

Folded notes

Cards

"Many years ago, Kate decided it was finally time to throw a soup-to-nuts dinner party. I designed the invitation—a poster showing the Heimlich maneuver—sealed with a sticker containing the words 'You're invited to Kate's **first** dinner party.'"

—Andy Spade

AS FOR INVITATIONS SENT BY FAX AND E-MAIL...

If you're too busy or late to get your invitations in the mail, then a telephone call is still preferable to either a fax or an e-mail. And so much more personal! (p.s. Don't leave a message on the answering machine.)

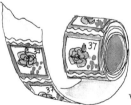

When you send out invitations with an RSVP, usually an additional ten to twenty percent more people will show up than actually reply. If you haven't asked for confirmations, you can expect about two-thirds of those you've asked.

DRESSING THE PART

"Being the hostess gives me an excuse to wear some of my most treasured clothes. And since I don't have to worry about going out into rain or snow, or having to walk anywhere, I can sidestep any consideration of weather or travel. So I bring out the high heels and as always, throw on splashes of color."

MY "RULES" FOR DRESS-UP

1. Wear my most favorite colors (and these change)

2. Great accessories . . . but edit, edit, edit!

3. Be comfortable

IT'S A PARTY—WEAR A HAT! WEAR SPARKLY COCKTAIL RINGS! WEAR A SMILE.

QUESTION
Whatever shall I wear?

ANSWER
Whatever you love.

As the hostess, you have the privilege of festooning yourself in swags of sparkly jewelry and Indian silks. Wear shoes that entice.

WHEN THE HANDS ON THE CLOCK MOVE FROM 9 AM TO 7 PM...

When you've been at the office all day and you don't have time to change before heading off to an event after work, consider wearing a "day to night" outfit—your best black trousers, perfect white shirt, loafers—and making minor but telling adjustments. Fling off the flats and put on shiny slingbacks with a big flower at the toe, add some dangly earrings, and perhaps an overscaled necklace.

Going to a party with 100 of your nearest and dearest? For the invite that reads "festive attire," reach into your closet and take a spin in something special, such as that backless dress in turquoise silk charmeuse you've been saving. Its moment has arrived.

THE VERSATILE SHEATH

A classic sheath is universal skim coating for any figure. Its forgiving silhouette is also ideal for nearly any occasion, from fancy to casual breezy. Accessories move the dress from a uniform to your own form.

YOUR JEWELRY—No jewelry better suits this dress than necklaces. Pearls are always acceptable, but instead of one strand wear many, go for a short, chunky necklace with a hard-to-miss pendant, or try something with pretty colored stones. Clusters of clear beads not only work with every color of dress or hair imaginable, they will become little orbs of shimmering beauty in candlelight.

YOUR SHOES—Turn up the volume here and go high, as in high heels. Be playful, be elegant, be dramatic...shoes with bows, rhinestones, flowers, in soft leather or in peau de soie (striped, no less) all lead you to the same destination—a party.

YOUR HANDBAG—Small and simple, small and fun, small and pretty. Whatever you do, leave your day purse at home and carry something that holds only the essentials.

THE GOOD HOSTESS

"A hostess is at her best when she's invisible performing duties,
such as getting another bottle of wine for the table.
I'm happiest when I'm not being noticed looking after my guests."

HELPFUL HINTS . . .

Preparation! Preparation! Preparation! The hostess who chants this mantra
(to herself, of course) will always be relaxed and have a fun evening.

Be showered and dressed an hour before you expect the first
guests to arrive. Even the most conscientious hostess will forget
this on her pre-party checklist.

Setting out your vases or favorite containers a f
ew days before your party helps reduce last-
minute worries. Check them for any lingering
water lines or spots. Dust with a soft cloth, if
needed. (To remove water lines on your vases,
soak them overnight in a solution of white
vinegar and warm water. A squeeze of lemon
helps, too.)

Do a last-minute check of closet hangers, hand towels, and ashtrays, if using.

Anticipate the comfort of your guests. Chances are they will appreciate your
well-trained pets, especially from afar. Cats will usually scamper off at the
sound of the doorbell. Dogs may need some persuading.

Even if you have servers at your cocktail party, be sure to pass
around a couple of hors d'oeuvre platters yourself. It's a good
way to mingle among your guests.

Once your guests begin arriving, get thee out of the kitchen! And
remember: avoid leaving your guests for longer than fifteen minutes.
They have come to be with you, not your veal scaloppine, no matter
how good it tastes.

FOREWARNED IS FOREARMED

Know your guests—and their tastes. Keep a journal of dinners you have given (the date, what was served, and who attended), and take special care to note each person's likes and dislikes. Indicating food allergies is a *must*.

"I FIND THAT CLEANING UP IS AN IMMEDIATE WAY TO END A PARTY. AS FOR THE DISHES, I ALWAYS SAY TO MY GUESTS WHO OFFER TO HELP, 'DON'T EVEN GO NEAR THEM!'"

A PARTICULARLY PLEASING PET

"On the subject of pets at parties, I can be perfectly egalitarian. My dog, Henry, is by my side, no matter where I am—at home, where he has free range, at the office, where he has free range, out shopping, where he has free range. In fact, Henry's never met a cocktail or dinner party that he didn't like. (Fortunately, all my friends know Henry and enjoy his company.) But if I didn't have Henry, would I worry about dogs overwhelming my guests? Perhaps."

Hospitality has long been associated with the pineapple, once valued as a rare fruit. The hostess who deco-rated her table with a pineapple signified the esteem in which she regarded her guests.

IS THERE A DIPLOMAT IN THE HOUSE?

Children and parties for grown-ups can be a delicate situation. You may want your children at your party, but will your guests? Here the hostess must use her best judgment and be both diplomat and parent. Good judgment is a must.

THE GOOD GUEST

"Being a good guest comes with experience, what I think of as trial by fire. For instance, I've learned that no matter how much I want to chat with my hostess, I'm supposed to leave her free to greet and mingle with everyone else. Or at least that's how I feel when I host a party, so I try to remember that when I'm someone's guest."

The kindest way to give flowers to your hostess is to have them sent ahead of time.

If the party is more self-serve than heavily catered, offer the hostess your help. If she declines (and shoos you from the kitchen) gracefully rejoin the party.

Mingling and making conversation is an art you can master . . . just by practicing.

Pet Etiquette: Never feed treats on the sly to someone else's pet, especially at a cocktail party. "People" food can upset a dog's digestion, and a dog who swallows a chicken wing can really bring a party to a halt.

The good guest has a sense of time—he or she knows when to arrive and, just as importantly, when to leave.

FASHIONABLY LATE

Time is more elastic when it comes to late arrivals at cocktail parties, but when invited to someone's home for dinner, keep in mind this timetable:

15 minutes—no questions asked

30 minutes—expect a raised eyebrow or two

45 minutes—you're fumbling at the goal line

60 minutes—consider yourself benched for the season and apologize profusely

TO SMOKE OR NOT TO SMOKE: "LET YOUR FRIENDS' PLEASED OR PAINED EXPRESSIONS WHEN YOU LIGHT UP BE YOUR GUIDE."

—AMY VANDERBILT

HOSTESS GIFTS I LIKE TO GIVE...

A case of wine ("I don't know anyone who doesn't like this.")

National Geographic Atlas of the World

A season's worth of tennis or golf balls

CDs—Introduce your hostess to new music, such as Sufjan Stevens, *Michigan*

A handful of your local nursery's best flowering bulbs—paperwhites or amaryllis—in a white pottery bowl for planting

Monopoly ("Still one of my favorites.")

Votives with special candles

Vintage interior design books (David Hicks, *Living with Design*, and Emily Post, *The Personality of a House* are must-haves)

A wooden bowl with ripe peaches, tied with a pale green ribbon

"I ADORE GIVING FLOWERS."

A sampling of miniature bottles of single-malt scotches, presented with a set of perfect shot glasses

"ANYTHING THAT'S NOT TOO SERIOUS!"

SURPRISES AND DISASTERS

"Talk about bending over backwards! Some years ago at a cocktail party
given by my parents one of their friends accidentally spilled a glass of red wine on
our white couch. The guest was horrified, but my mother just laughed and said
not to worry. And then she tossed her glass of wine on the couch, too.
It immediately diffused the tension and made everyone feel comfortable."

REMOVING RED WINE

Now that your guests have left, it's time to
quickly tackle red-wine stains. If the tablecloth
or napkin fabric is sturdy, coat the area with
salt and rub in well; allow to sit for five
minutes. Then stretch the stained area over a
heatproof bowl and secure with a rubber band.
From at least a foot high, continuously pour
hot water over the stain until it is gone.

"Occasionally we find ourselves with
the 'UNEXPECTED GUEST.'
Naturally, we always make room and
are all smiles. But secretly I wonder
why our guest didn't call ahead."

A "BORROWED" COCKTAIL NAPKIN

What do you do when you inadvertently
stuff your used *cloth* cocktail napkin in your
pocket? (My husband occasionally does this.)
Wash it, iron it, and return it with a note
and small tin of nuts.

The most discreet Band-Aid for a BROKEN WINEGLASS or plate at a party is its speediest possible replacement. The hostess applies the best balm with a reassuring smile and words that gloss over the incident.

THE GUEST WHO WON'T SAY GOOD-BYE

Gesture and innuendo are the most accommodating ways to unseat an unaccommodating guest. When he or she drinks, you abstain. Fob off fatigue on your spouse. Start rounding up the used glasses, plates, and napkins.

TOO MUCH WINE

If your soused guest is merry and fun, then who cares? But if your guest starts to snarl and curl his or her lip, then out the door!

"One of my friends told me about the time she seriously splurged on a dress for a black-tie opening at the Museum of Modern Art. She walked in—feeling pretty darn special—and she saw that among her group of friends another woman had on THE SAME DRESS. For a moment she said she felt crushed. But then she decided to make the best of it and exchange 'compliments' with the other woman. What else can you do?"

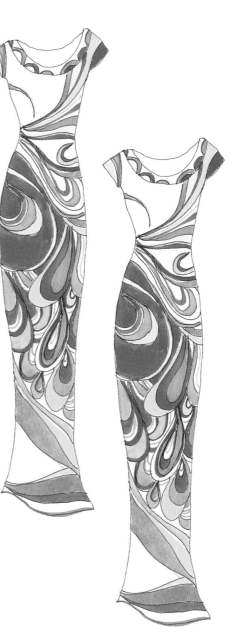

AVALANCHE À TABLE

Just as your guest shakes out some salt on his plate, the top comes off and lands in his mashed potatoes—along with most of the salt. Before your guest struggles to cover his embarrassment, swiftly come to his aid with a quick apology and a fresh plate of food. Deftly remove the offending salt shaker.

TROUBLE IN PARADISE

It can happen in a flash: the newlyweds at your dinner for six get into an argument at the table. What can't be ignored must be addressed with as much grace and diplomacy as possible. Suggest that the couple briefly excuse themselves while they sort things out. Dinner should continue apace.

Even the most gregarious person can find a SURPRISE BIRTHDAY PARTY daunting. Before you shoot a potentially unsavory aside to the party planner, consider that the host has given you the party out of friendship and love. Blow out your candles. Enjoy yourself.

CHOCOLATE SOUP

Back in the kitchen, your soufflé didn't fall, but it didn't exactly rise, either. Just the same, all that chocolate tastes pretty good. Serve it in pretty soup bowls with spoons and a smile.

Tried 'n True Party Standards

Cocktail Parties · Pre-Party Preparations · Mixed Drinks

Shake, Stir, Pour, and Serve · The Perfect Martini

Champagne and Cognac · Wine is Divine · Beer is a Beverage Too

Hors d'Oeuvres · À la Carte, À Table, and Catering

Dinner Parties · Dinner Party Checklist · Special Dinner Parties

The Art of the Toast · Dinner Party Trivia · Weekend Parties

For the Ideal Guest Room · Weekend Activities in the Country

COCKTAIL PARTIES

"If I had to choose, I'd say that cocktail parties are all-around the most fun to have. I'm surrounded by good friends and the party gives me a chance to invite new acquaintances as well, which I might be less inclined to do at a small sit-down dinner. Then there's the fact that a cocktail party gives me an excuse to decorate our place with votives and flowers everywhere. I prefer when the party is catered (and I do think that a simple outfit is best here) because then I'm freer to talk with our guests. To be perfectly honest, my idea of fun is not running in and out of the kitchen."

PRE-PARTY PREPARATIONS

☐ Chill any juices, mixers, and bottled water

☐ Check for water spots on glasses

☐ Have a good pair of ice tongs handy (it keeps the ice bucket finger-free)

☐ If you plan on serving a couple specialty drinks such as Piña Coladas or Negronis, consider making pitchers in advance (and be sure to ice the drinks well when you serve them)

☐ When serving wine, it's a good idea to have a red and a white that will not dominate the hors d'oeuvres

☐ Open roughly half the bottles before the party and set them out, partially corked, before your guests arrive (be sure to ice the white)

☐ Slice lemons and limes, set out cocktail onions for martinis

☐ Stragglers will appreciate a cup of coffee before they leave, so set up your coffeemaker and cups before the party begins

"DARLING LITTLE WATER" IS THE LITERAL TRANSLATION OF VODKA.

PRACTICE MAKES PERFECT
Good training for the home bartender is perfecting the concoction of your signature drink.

DON'T CLAM UP...
IT'S ONLY A COCKTAIL PARTY

The gifted conversationalist is big in demand but short on supply at most cocktail parties. For reasons not fully fathomed, even the simplest of topics can be run into the ground in mere seconds: your occupation (interesting to a point), are you married/single, do you have children (yes/no questions are fast burnouts), and of course the weather (always boring). Even if you lack a silver tongue, you needn't avoid all comers and head for the canapés.

WHEN MAKING COCKTAIL
PARTY SMALL TALK...

Keep a sense of humor

Abandon false cheer

Introduce yourself to others

Be interested and do ask questions

Look for common interests

Mingle, mingle, mingle

Skip politics but stay with movies, restaurants, or travel destinations

Beware of dispensing T.M.I.—too much information

Be confident

BAR BASICS

Vodka
Gin
Scotch
Whiskey
Rum
Dry Vermouth
Sweet Vermouth
Bourbon
Tequila
Rose's lime juice
Triple sec
Club soda
Tonic
Tomato juice
(or Bloody Mary mix)
Horseradish
Angostura bitters
Grenadine
Cocktail olives
Cocktail onions
Lemons and limes
Stirrers, shakers, and strainers

In Barbados, rum used to be known as "kill divill."

PAPER UMBRELLAS ARE A
FUN TOUCH, ESPECIALLY
FOR A CARIBBEAN-
THEMED BRUNCH.

MIXED DRINKS

Once you've mastered basic cocktail concoctions (practice, practice, practice),
then you can work on perfecting the "art of the pour."

VODKA

BLACK RUSSIAN
2 oz vodka, 1 oz Kahlua

COSMOPOLITAN
2 oz citron vodka, ¼ oz triple sec, ¼ oz lime juice, ¼ oz cranberry juice

SEA BREEZE
1½ oz vodka, 2 oz cranberry juice, 2 oz fresh grapefruit juice

SCREWDRIVER
2 oz vodka, 5 oz fresh orange juice

BLOODY MARY
2 oz vodka, 4 oz tomato juice, ½ tsp horseradish, Worcestershire, Tabasco, salt, pepper, celery salt,
celery stalk for garnish

HARVEY WALLBANGER
2 oz vodka, 4 oz orange juice, 1 oz Galliano

BULLSHOT
2 oz vodka, 4 oz chilled beef bouillon, Worcestershire, Tabasco

GIN

GIMLET
2 oz gin, ½ oz lime juice, lime wedge garnish

TOM COLLINS
2 oz gin, 1 oz fresh lemon juice, 1 tsp sugar, 3 oz club soda

CLASSIC MARTINI
3 oz gin, splash vermouth, olives or cocktail onions for garnish

NEGRONI (DRY)
1 oz gin, 1 oz dry vermouth, 1 oz Campari, lime garnish

SHADY GROVE
1½ oz gin, juice of ½ lemon, 1 tsp powdered sugar, ginger beer

RUM

BOSTON SIDECAR
¾ oz rum, ¾ oz brandy, ¾ oz triple sec, juice of ½ lime

DAIQUIRI (FROZEN)
2 oz light rum, 1 tbs triple sec, 1½ oz fresh lime juice, 1 tsp sugar, 1 cup crushed ice

MOJITO
1 tsp sugar, ¼ oz fresh lime juice, 1½ oz silver dry Havana club rum, fresh mint, 2 oz sparkling water

PIÑA COLADA
2 oz light rum, 2 oz cream of coconut, 4 oz pineapple juice, fresh pineapple garnish

SCOTCH

ROB ROY
2 oz scotch, ¾ oz dry vermouth, ¾ oz sweet vermouth

RUSTY NAIL
¾ oz scotch, ¼ oz Drambuie

TEQUILA

MARGARITA
1½ oz tequila, ½ oz triple sec, 1 oz fresh lemon or lime juice

FROZEN MANGO MARGARITA
3 oz blanco tequila, 1½ cups peeled and diced ripe mango, 1 oz Cointreau, 2 oz fresh lime juice, 3 tbs superfine sugar, 2 cups crushed ice

TEQUILA AND TONIC
3 oz tequila, ¼ lime, 4 oz tonic, lime garnish

TEQUILA SUNRISE
2 oz tequila, 4 oz fresh orange juice, 1 oz grenadine

SHAKE, STIR, POUR . . . AND SERVE

When it comes to making drinks, a few pointers will help you better manage the basics and ensure that your guests enjoy their cocktails.

- A "stiff" drink is not a good drink—pouring more liquor than is called for in a classic cocktail is never a good idea. The taste is "off," and so, too, is your sodden guest, who will not appreciate your "generosity" the next day.

- Learn what "just a touch" and "a splash" mean. The drinker who requests this is probably pretty particular.

- Take care not to burst your bubbles—when a cocktail includes tonic or club soda, avoid overly stirring, which may dissipate the bubbles.

- Shaking a drink calls for balance and poise—when using a two-part classic shaker combine the ingredients in the beaker (stainless steel or glass), then cup the top over the vessel and shake well, up and down rather than left to right. (If you're too vigorous, ice shavings may wind up in your drink.) Pour out using a metal strainer.

- You can never have too much ice—ice in a home freezer can spoil and pick up food odors, so for the freshest of beverages, buy bags of ice. If you want to make your own ice, do so within days of your party. Whether you buy it or make it, be sure that it's been made with distilled or purified water.

- It's one thing to request a dirty martini, but no martini drinker ever wants one that's *cloudy*. To prevent this from happening, always *stir* the liquor and ice. Shaking may cause little splinters of ice to get into the drink, which then melt and "fog" your martini.

- Top off the head of a beer before serving your guest.

COCKTAIL CONCOCTIONS

American Beauty Cocktail
Bloody Mary
Boston Sidecar
Damn-the-Weather Cocktail
Dark 'n Stormy
Gin Thing
Income Tax Cocktail
Kiss in the Dark
Magnolia Maiden
Manhattan
Margarita
Martini, Martini, Martini
Pink Squirrel
Ritz Fizz
Rusty Nail
Singapore Sling
Stinger
Thoroughbred Cooler
Vodka and Tonic
Whiskey Daisy
Widow's Kiss
Zombie
. . . and beware the trendy drink

ERNEST HEMINGWAY'S DEATH-IN-THE-AFTERNOON COCKTAIL

Invite a friend over.
Pour 1 jigger of absinthe into each champagne glass.
Fill with champagne.
Drink 3, 4, or 5 of these very slowly
while discussing fly-fishing.

BENNY GOODMAN'S ADMIRAL COCKTAIL

1 part bourbon, 2 parts dry vermouth, and
juice of ¼ lemon. Shake well with ice cubes.
Pour and garnish with a twist of lemon.

VIRGIN CRANBERRY COOLER

Treat yourself to a cranberry cooler after a game of
badminton with your nephew.

5 oz cranberry juice
½ tbs lime juice
Club soda
Lime garnish

Add the juices to a Collins glass filled with ice. Top with club soda, stir, and garnish with a twist of
lime. Substituting 2 ounces of vodka for the club soda will make this a drink for grown-ups.
(And then it will be known as a Cape Codder.)

APRÈS SKI COCKTAILS

Hot Buttered Rum
Racing Stripe
Warming Hut
Gin Garland
Ski Blazer

SNOWMAN

2 oz light rum

2 oz lemon
juice

1 tsp
simple syrup

3 pineapple chunks

Combine ingredients
in a blender. Add a
small amount of
cracked ice and blend
until drink is mixed and
chilled. Serve in a chilled cocktail glass.

CHEERS HEARD
AROUND THE WORLD

Irish	"Slante!"
Japanese	"Kampai!"
Russian	"Na zdrovia!"
Zulu	"Oogy wawa!"

FOR FROZEN DRINKS,
A BLENDER IS
A MUST-HAVE.

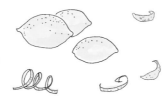

The first lemons were
planted in A.D. 4 by the
writer Palladius. Two
thousand years later,
it's a citrus we never
tire of.

THE PERFECT MARTINI

"For years I've had a special feeling for martinis. In *The Thin Man* films, martinis were served in small glasses, with the most darling little stem. To me, the size was ideal. Today, I think most of the glasses are much too big—by the time you've taken two sips it's already warm! The best martini I've ever had was at Cipriani, here in New York, where it was served in a glass that looked like a votive. The votive was chilled and frosted all over, and the vodka was also kept in the freezer. They poured in the cold vodka, added just a drop of vermouth, and set a toothpick speared with olives across the glass. Now that's what I call a martini. If I were to serve martinis, that's the way I'd go because the vodka isn't hot by the time you finish. You need to sip a martini slowly, so you want to make sure it stays cold."

"GENTLEMEN, SHED YOUR CHAPEAUX!"

—NICK CHARLES, THE THIN MAN

"I LOVE TO DRINK MARTINIS,
TWO AT THE VERY MOST
THREE, I'M UNDER THE TABLE
FOUR, I'M UNDER THE HOST."

—DOROTHY PARKER

MARTINIS

"My father insists that a
real martini is only made
with gin. So if you want a
vodka martini, he says you
have to specifically request
vodka. Hmm . . ."

IT'S A TOSS-UP

James Bond may have immortalized the perfect
martini, but Raymond Chandler's sleuth,
Philip Marlowe, was a gimlet man, beginning
with his first taste of the concoction
in *The Long Goodbye* (1953).

CHAMPAGNE AND COGNAC: ALWAYS IN STYLE

"Champagne is one of those drinks that's always special. Nothing gives sparkle to an occasion like a flute filled with delicious champagne. I love serving it at our parties, especially when guests are first arriving and settling in."

DEFINING CHAMPAGNE

BRUT=very dry; the most popular style of champagne

EXTRA SEC, EXTRA DRY=fairly dry

SEC=moderately sweet

DEMI-SEC=distinctly sweet

DOUX=very sweet, more like a dessert wine

DECODING COGNAC

V=very

S=special

O=old

P=pale

F=fine

X=extra

CHAMPAGNE BY THE BOTTLE

SPLIT=6.3 fluid oz (roughly 1 glass)

HALF BOTTLE=37.5 cl, 12.7 fluid oz

BOTTLE=75 cl, 25.4 fluid oz

MAGNUM=2 bottles, 1.5 litres

JEROBOAM=4 bottles, 3 litres

CHAMPAGNE GOES TO THE MOVIES

For the musical *Gigi* (1958) composers Lerner and Loewe wrote the charming song "The Night They Invented Champagne." The movie is based on a short story by Colette and stars Leslie Caron and Maurice Chevalier.

In *Letter from an Unknown Woman* (1948), the Max Ophuls classic with Joan Fontaine and Louis Jourdan, the doomed love affair is reprised briefly when one of the lovers says, "Champagne tastes much better after midnight, don't you agree?"

WINE IS DIVINE

"Now that I've decided I'm too old to have martinis, my instinctive drink of choice
is wine. And what a choice! With all the different reds and whites, I'm always
game to try a new label or vintage, though I do admit to having a crush on red wine,
especially from Napa Valley. In the past, Andy and I used to buy wine on an
as-needed basis, but either our needs grew or we wised up, because now we
always try to have a couple of cases on hand. It's more economical too, and I'm
happy when I can buy something and be thrifty at the same time."

ENJOY YOURSELF

What happy homework it is to educate yourself about wine.
Begin by selecting moderately priced wines and trying a
variety of them. If you don't know much, don't hesitate to
ask your wine merchant for suggestions (and don't hold
back about your budget, either). Last point: Trust your
taste buds—if you don't like the wine, chances are it's not
right for you, or perhaps it's not right, period.

TASTING AND TALKING ABOUT WINE

AROMA—As simple as how a wine smells, such as floral, herbaceous, or spicy.

BODY—Not about size but about the richness of a wine, what is uniquely referred to as its viscosity.

CLEAN—If you understand the meaning of this word, then you have a keen grasp of good wine. A
well-made wine that is free of dirt or spoilage is described as being clean.

COLOR—In wine parlance, color equals quality. Just as color is one of the key standards for judging
a ruby or emerald, so the same holds true for wine. Color indicates everything from the method of
production to the body of the wine.

FRUITY—A younger wine tastes more of the grape, and hence is said to be fruity.

OAKY—In contrast to fruity wines, for example, oaky wines impart their fermentation in oak barrels.
A good oaky wine has vanilla or wood notes, but not in overabundance.

TANNIN—That pucker-in-your-mouth feeling comes from young reds with a lot of tannin.

CONSIDER THE GRAPE

CLASSIC REDS

Beaujolais

Bordeaux

Cabernet Sauvignon

Merlot

Montrachet

Pinot Noir

Syrah

Zinfandel

CLASSIC WHITES

Chardonnay

Chenin Blanc

Gewürztraminer

Muscat

Riesling

Roussanne

Sauternes

Sauvignon Blanc (includes Pouilly-Fumé and Sancerre)

Viognier

TEMPERATURE CONTROL

WHITE WINE—serve between 43–55 degrees. Best served cool, not icy.

RED WINE—serve between 55–65 degrees, or what is known as "cellar tempera-ture." Room temperature is considered too warm.

WINE AND FOOD

Wine meets its match in the food department, for perhaps with the exception of cereal or marshmallows, there is a wine for nearly every food and every occasion. Just as you can now wear white after Labor Day, so you no longer have to subscribe to the traditional rule of pairing red wine with meat and white with fish. The art of mating wine with food is truly the basis of all fine entertaining.

CHICKEN—It's the perfect blank canvas for wine, but you have to consider the preparation and the sauce. If it's a tomato sauce, think red, but if it's lemony with herbs, then a nice clean Chardonnay is a wise choice.

FISH—Pinot Noir, for example, is an inspired companion to salmon, arctic char, or tuna. But for delicate fish such as halibut or Dover sole, think white and light.

RED MEAT—Red with red still works best; what varies is the selection (Zinfandel, Bordeaux, Cabernet Sauvignon) and your own inclination toward either lighter or more full-bodied reds.

PASTA—As with chicken, it's the sauce that rules. Consider a Zinfandel with a spicy ragù or a Chenin Blanc with something creamy such as Spaghetti Carbonara. (As for pizza, chianti is a must.)

DESSERT—Allowance should be made for dessert wines, the "noble rot" of vitrified grapes. Vin Santo, Sauternes, or Trockenbeerenauslese are delicious with nut or fruit desserts, such as a homey peach cobbler or elegant hazelnut tart.

BEER IS A BEVERAGE TOO

"I love beer. I'm a beer freak, probably because of the great Pilsner glass.
A bartender will take a Pilsner glass, fill it all the way up without any foam, and then
hand it to you—perfect and cold. So when we have in friends, I always serve them
beer in Pilsner glasses. Unless we're doing a barbecue and then no guy wants a glass,
just the bottle, thank you very much. And I stay away from canned beer. It makes me
think of the Indy 500 or something. All that metal!"

AROUND THE WORLD WITH BEER

"I'm pretty crazy for foreign beers. If we're going to throw a party
where we're having beer, I think it's fun to have different foreign
beers. I must say I particularly like having Tecate beer with
Mexican food and a Tsing Tao or Sapporo with sushi."

MEXICO
Pacifico, Dos Equis,
Tecate, Negra Modelo

GERMANY
Beck's, Holsten Pils,
Erdinger Weissbier

CANADA
Labatts,
Moosehead

ENGLAND
Black Sheep Ale,
Morlands Speckled Hen,
Young's Double Chocolate Stout

AUSTRALIA
Coopers Stout,
Foster's Ice

IRELAND
Oyster Stout,
Porterhouse Red

HOLLAND
Grolsch

BELGIUM
Chimay Blue,
Liefmans Gluhkriek

CZECH REPUBLIC
Pilsner Urquell,
Zubr, Yelkopovivcky

USA
Brooklyn Lager, Casco Bay
Pilsner, Anchor Steam,
Rolling Rock

SCOTLAND
Maclay's Oat Malt Stout,
Fraoch Heather Ale

WHEN YOUR COCKTAIL OF CHOICE IS BEER...

REDNECK MIMOSA

½ pint fresh orange juice
½ pint wheat beer or golden lager
Thin rounds of orange for garnish

Fill a glass with the juice and add the lager.
Add orange slices.

SEPARATING THE WHEAT FROM THE HOPS...

LAGER

The "white wine" of the beer kingdom, with
a slight maltiness and overall lightness in
flavor and body. Serve a lager-style beer
(such as a Pilsner) with hors d'oeuvres or
with seafood and chicken.

ALE

They run the color and taste gamut from pale to amber to red, with each hue having a more pronounced
flavor, depth, and complexity. Pale ales contain dried malts, whereas amber and red ales are made with
roasted malts. Foodwise, pale ale is ideal with chicken and grilled burgers, amber suits salmon or pork,
and a rich red ale complements a hearty dish of venison or lamb.

PORTER

Not a steak, but a richly malted beer that is great with steak. You can spot a porter by its dark brown color.

BOCK

Aptly named, for in German *bock* means "strong beer," and this beer tends to be a "big" beer, full
of flavor, body, some bitterness, and a higher alcohol content than other styles of beer. Think of it as
a strong cup of coffee, and offer it with a rich dessert.

STOUT

A major taste with lots of body and flavor, and a deep near-black color to match. If bock is coffee,
then stout is espresso. Perfect with dessert or enjoy solo at the end of a meal.

LAGER AND LIME

1 tsp Rose's lime juice
1 tsp fresh lime juice
8 oz cold golden lager
Lime wedge for garnish

Combine the Rose's and fresh lime juice.
Stir in the lager and garnish with a slice of lime.

HORS D'OEUVRES

"First and foremost, hors d'oeuvres should be delicious. I think that's the most important thing. I want someone to look at the food and think *yum*. There you are, you're having a glass of wine and you're starving and then boom— you see a really delicious-looking hors d'oeuvre and you think to yourself, 'Oh, please... this is something I want.' Then you have to figure out a place to put your drink. As a hostess, you have to take that into account."

MY KIND OF HORS D'OEUVRES

"Whenever I'm having a party, I explain to a caterer that I think the food should be filling, but also easy to eat and beautifully presented. I like when the hors d'oeuvres have a sense of humor so that the whole thing isn't too serious. But not gimmicky. And I never want anyone to think the food is silly."

"When a party is casual, don't be a slacker—make an effort."

"Andy and I love pigs-in-a-blanket. But not just any pigs-in-a-blanket. The traditional ones made by William Poll are the best—they're homemade, straightforward yet delicious and flaky. The other thing is, when you bite into one you believe someone made it, you sense the hand."

"Eleni makes little pastry cups that she turns into a BLT. She takes the little cups and fills them with chopped bacon, lettuce, and tomatoes. Everything's perfectly chopped and blended. They're bite-size, and when you have one you really feel as though you're having a BLT. Which you are."

"Hors d'oeuvres should be bite-size. I think it's hard to bite into something with a napkin and a drink already in your hand. That's why I like mini foods, which you can just pop in."

"Much as I love special party foods, I'm also a Triscuits-and-cheese girl. But I wouldn't dare let them seem ordinary. I'd want them to be special, so I'd serve them on a decorative or unusual platter."

"What do I shy away from? For one thing, I'm not a big buffet fan. Platters of shrimp make me start to worry about all those shrimp getting just a bit too warm. And I think baked hams are delicious, although they seem a little daunting to me. Besides, they never look very appetizing halfway through the evening. I'd take a skip on nuts too. Though Andy loves them."

"We rely a great deal on Peter Callahan, who's an amazing caterer. We describe the type of event we're having and he comes up with the most remarkable foods. And they're small, which I like."

PETER'S SPECIALTIES

Frites in a cone — five-inch-long French fries wrapped in plain paper cones. Served in clear lucite trays with holes for each cone.

Pigs-in-a-blanket — smoked salmon and black bread in the shape of pigs with a bellyband of wasabi caviar

Mini tuna burgers — sushi-like tuna "burger" served on a poppy seed bun (the size of a quarter) with sun-dried tomato, cucumber, wasabi, and chèvre

Caviar "ice cream" cones — potato cones filled with crème fraîche and topped with sturgeon caviar

Mini strawberry-rhubarb ice cream cones

Cotton candy lollipops — deep pink, of course

PETER'S PINK LEMONADE WITH KIWI

À LA CARTE, À TABLE, AND CATERING

"For me, a huge variable when I'm planning to have a party is whether I am also doing the cooking or having the evening catered. Then there's the fact that sometimes the event simply is casual, and I don't want everyone to feel they're at some fancy feast. I find that buffets and finger foods for cocktails work best when your gathering is more than a dozen people; above that number, you're only limited by the size of your home and your budget. Serving food is much more forgiving than when you're having a sit-down dinner for eight. Caterers and college students to help with serving can be life-savers to the busy hostess."

DO-IT-YOURSELF VS HIRING A CATERER

Whether you decide to do everything yourself or hire a caterer, the look, tempo, and mood of the event is uniquely your vision. The caterer is an extension of your taste, not a substitute or stand-in.

SOCIAL DILEMMA #437

There it is, the last potato chip, and it's sitting in a bowl in plain view. You know you want that chip, yet you don't want to seem as if you can't control yourself and have everyone think you're being piggy. On the other hand, why should someone else have the chip that you want? Before you do a stealth motion and bravely take that chip, stop and ask yourself, "Why is it there? What sort of person would take the last chip? Is this a metaphor about Life?"

"HENRY SAYS THAT HORS D'OEUVRES ARE HIS FAVORITE SNACK FOOD AT PARTIES. HE'S EGALITARIAN AND LIKES THEM ALL, EXCEPT PERHAPS ASPARAGUS SPEARS."

A FEW FOOD NOTES

Always err on the side of generosity
when planning hors d'oeuvres.

Your guests will eat more in cool
weather, and less in warm weather.

The larger the gathering, the fewer
hors d'oeuvres consumed by each person.

WHEN THE HORS D'OEUVRES
ARE SWEET...

"I don't see why you can't pass dessert hors
d'oeuvres. If you put them on a table, there's a
feeding frenzy, which doesn't look very nice.
Besides, it's a gentle way of letting people know that
the evening is winding down, or at least officially."

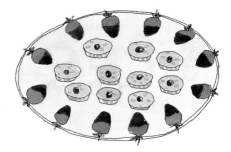

HOW DO YOU END A COCKTAIL PARTY?

"I'D HIT THE BREAKER SWITCH AND TURN
OFF ALL THE LIGHTS AND MUSIC."

—ANDY SPADE

DINNER PARTIES

"I think it's nice to make even a simple meal seem special, whether the guests
are your closest friends or people you're getting to know. Certainly I'd never want our
good friends to think we take them for granted, so even if a dinner is planned
with just one other couple, I want to make sure we have fresh flowers and candles and that
the evening is festive and fun. It's all about making an effort, taking the time to
consider what your guests will enjoy. Whether we use our good china or something more
casual, I try to keep the atmosphere from becoming too serious, too la-di-da
grown-up. Laughter is on every menu at our home! Much as I love to entertain
and have friends over rather than go out, I don't see myself standing in the kitchen
for hours. Then there are the nights when Andy and I have the occasional 'date'—
just the two of us, popcorn, and an old movie."

HORS D'OEUVRES VARIÉS

Smiles and Greetings

POTAGE

Hospitality

ROTIS

*A Solid Understanding of the
Topics of the Day*

SALAD

Conversation with Sauce Piquante

BEVERAGES

*Cocktail—A Spicy Bit of Gossip
A Punch of Mirth and Understanding*

DEMI-TASSE

"And a Pleasant Time Was Had by All"

DINNER PARTY CHECKLIST

You may not need to do everything listed below when preparing for
and hosting a dinner party, so pick and choose what's most helpful.

- ☐ Create the menu
- ☐ Consider the table decorations
- ☐ Shopping list for food
- ☐ Shopping list for drinks, lemons and limes, ice
- ☐ Shopping list for flowers, candles, special lighting
- ☐ Choose music for the evening
- ☐ Select table linens—clean and iron, if necessary
- ☐ Select glassware, dishes, and flatware as well as special serving pieces
- ☐ Make arrangements for guest coats

- ☐ Cook!
- ☐ Set the table
- ☐ Arrange the centerpiece
- ☐ Prepare lighting (votives, tapers, other candles)
- ☐ Set up the bar, prepare drinks
- ☐ Turn on the music (and pour yourself a drink)
- ☐ The guests begin to arrive . . . pass hors d'oeuvres, serve drinks

- ☐ Dinner!
- ☐ Dessert!
- ☐ More drinks, coffee, small candies
- ☐ Say good night and head for a well-deserved sleep

In Harold Pinter's play
The Dinner Party, no
dinner ever actually
takes place.

SPECIAL DINNER PARTIES

"Over the years we've given special dinners, and we've been to some that stay in my mind. One recent favorite was an evening where my friend Eleni created a dinner based on lemons. She set the table with lemon-colored napkins and placemats that were embroidered with little lemons. She even found napkin rings that looked like lemons. The candles were striped—yellow and white. And the menu was really fun: Greek roasted potatoes with lemon, lemon chicken, asparagus with lemon vinaigrette. The best moment was when she served dessert—she'd scooped out real lemons and filled them with lemon sorbet and placed lemon-shaped cookies on top."

BBQ

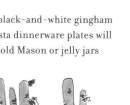

"A classic barbecue picnic or dinner is always loads of fun. There's something about the down-home food and country music that makes me smile. And with something this traditional, it's okay to get a little corny."

TABLE SETTING

Instead of using the standard red-and-white checked gingham, use tiny black-and-white gingham for your tablecloth and bright red cotton napkins as an accent. White Fiesta dinnerware plates will keep the look of the table clean and graphic. If you want to go all out, use old Mason or jelly jars for your drinks.

CENTERPIECE

White cylinder candles in three or four different heights clustered tightly at the center of the table look terrific surrounded by several little terra-cotta pots containing miniature cacti. Dream-case scenario: find miniature cacti with tiny red blossoms.

MENU

- ☐ Spicy Coleslaw
- ☐ Heartburn Salad
- ☐ Watermelon Rind Pickles
- ☐ Kansas City–Style Spareribs
- ☐ Grilled Chicken-and-Fennel Sausage
- ☐ Fresh Strawberries
- ☐ Popsicles

MUSIC

- ☐ *Timeless: Hank Williams Tribute*, Various Artists
- ☐ *Heartbreaker*, Ryan Adams
- ☐ *The Sun Years*, Johnny Cash

BUSY-IN-THE-CITY DINNER PARTY

"We all have busy schedules these days. Yet I find gathering friends for a fun dinner on nearly any night of the week is worth the effort. You don't have to go to great lengths, unless you have time—especially if you're inviting close friends who just want to catch up. (Andy and I have had impromptu dinner parties where we serve Mexican food from down the street.) With just a bit of planning, you can create a memorable evening of fun and conversation."

TABLE SETTING

"Whether you're having guests over on a weeknight or for the weekend, don't make yourself crazy chasing down all sorts of extra bits for the table. Pull out your favorite plates. I have a set that I love. It has a geometric multicolored trim in my favorite colors—pink, green, coral, and yellow. I like to use a white tablecloth for clarity, along with simple napkins. For this kind of meal, I might choose a wide green grosgrain ribbon as a napkin ring, pull out my day-to-day flatware, spiff up the table with gold-trimmed glassware, and call it a party. If I have the time, I'll pick up special chocolates or single-wrapped candies to set above each place setting as a treat."

CENTERPIECE

"Since I like to keep these parties easy-breezy—I'd rather have more time to banter with my friends—I select two dozen flowers that a) are in season and b) pick up one of the colors in my plates. In the spring, I'll buy fuchsia peonies or hydrangeas. Fall is a bit more difficult, but I can often find bunches of berries in pink or coral. A low vase of abundant flowers and a multitude of votive candles are perfectly complemented by crystal glasses showing off the gorgeous glow of great red wine."

MENU

- ☐ Slabs of Parmesan Cheese
- ☐ Enormous Tossed Salad
- ☐ Fresh Pasta with Three Kinds of Mushrooms
- ☐ Compote of Sliced Nectarines and Blueberries, topped with roasted almonds

MUSIC

- ☐ *If You're Feeling Sinister*, Belle and Sebastian
- ☐ *Hunky Dory*, David Bowie
- ☐ *United*, Phoenix

HARVEST DINNER

"I absolutely love the fall season. While everyone else is lamenting the end of summer, I'm thrilled to be putting on a cozy sweater (sometimes I snatch one of Andy's) and tweed coat, and gearing up for the holidays. A harvest dinner is such a warm, celebratory way to welcome autumn. And the menu? Hearty, delicious, and really filling."

TABLE SETTING

Rich chocolate brown accented by pinks and reds is dreamy. For the tablecloth, brown linen can easily be trimmed with raspberry pink ribbon or seam binding. Keep to white china, but give it some color by placing a pomegranate in the center of each plate. The ideal napkin for this setting is oversized white linen with a simple embroidered motif in pink or red. Polish off the table with clear wine and water glasses, but serve champagne in a red crystal champagne bowl to start or finish. For this dinner, pull out your best heirloom sterling silver.

CENTERPIECE

A large but low vase (take your pick—glass, silver, or ceramic) brimming with pink and red flowers is beautiful on this table. Wine-colored dahlias, pink and red ranunculus, plump red roses, and branches of berries cut short so they nestle within the blossoms is a dazzling combination. On either side of the centerpiece, place two of the longest, most graceful white taper candles you can find in small silver candle holders. The four tall candles soaring over the red and pink flowers make for a stunning centerpiece.

MENU

- ☐ Butternut Squash and Corn Chowder with Spicy Popcorn Garnish
- ☐ Roast Chicken with Carrots, Onions, and Garlic
- ☐ Cinnamon Apple Sauce
- ☐ Twice-Baked Potatoes
- ☐ Devil's Food Cake served with fresh whipped cream
- ☐ Apple Cider and Sparkling Cider

MUSIC

- ☐ *Insignificance*, Jim O'Rourke
- ☐ *Let It Be*, The Beatles
- ☐ *Silver and Gold*, Neil Young

SUMMER DINNER

"Warm summer nights provide the ideal setting for easy dinner parties. Andy and I love to entertain at our beach house. He's a sport and shops for basic fixings or swings by our local fish market. While he's out, I pick a basket of flowers from our backyard and work on the table. Later on I mix up a batch of cocktails for our guests."

TABLE SETTING

The combination of orange, yellow, and white makes for a crisp-looking table. A white linen tablecloth and napkins are a welcoming foundation for great lemony yellow plates, old or new. Put flower buds from your centerpiece in votive glasses and place one at every setting.

CENTERPIECE

Place a mix of loosely arranged flowers—sweet peas, daisies, white peonies, white and yellow poppies—in a large clear bubble bowl at the center of the table. Surround the vase with green glass votive holders containing white candles. Set additional votives randomly around the table. The more the better when it comes to candles, especially when dining outside. The table will sparkle.

MENU

- ☐ Cherrystone Clams, Mignonette Sauce
- ☐ Poached Salmon with Homemade Green Goddess Dressing
- ☐ Baked Fingerling Potatoes
- ☐ Sugarsnap Peas with Lemon and Fresh Mint
- ☐ Ice Cream Sandwiches (chocolate mint, strawberry, French vanilla)

MUSIC

- ☐ *Wildflowers*, Tom Petty
- ☐ *Mermaid Avenue*, Billy Bragg and Wilco
- ☐ *Central Reservation*, Beth Orton

THE ART OF THE TOAST

"My preference is to listen to someone give a toast, rather than have to give one myself. Over the years, I can say that short is good, wit combined with sincerity is even better. Put-downs, no matter how amusingly stated, always make me squirm."

FOR A GRACIOUS TOAST

Make use of eloquence, wit, and whimsy

Brevity is best—be brief, stay simple

Be yourself

Stand when making a toast

Be prepared—a toast is a miniature speech. Know your lines, craft your salutation

Exit—it's always good to know when to stop . . . and take your seat!

THE GUEST OF HONOR IS ALWAYS FIRST TOASTED BY THE HOST.

A gentle tap on a wine or water glass is international code for a toast.

WINEGLASSES

Clear is the kindest choice for wine, which deserves to be seen in its own hues and natural characteristics.

By the early 1800s, offering a toast at the table was both good manners and a way of enlivening the evening.

DINNER PARTY TRIVIA

"Of course I think that we've given or gone to great parties over the years, but whenever I read about parties from the past, they always sound so alluring. I confess that I take mental notes about these parties and try to incorporate little bits into our own dinners. Old movies also charm me and give me little ideas here and there."

PARTIES WE WISH WE'D ATTENDED...

Grace Kelly's Scorpio-themed 40th birthday party in Monaco

Truman Capote's Black-and-White masked ball for Katharine Graham

Gary and Rocky Cooper's at-home sing-alongs, with Judy Garland, Sammy Davis, Jr., and Louis Armstrong

Andy Warhol's "Fifty Most Beautiful People" party at the Factory, Spring 1968

Any White House State Dinner given by President and Mrs. Kennedy

"THE LAST AMERICAN PARTY"

When Truman Capote, buoyant and newly wealthy from his bestselling *In Cold Blood*, announced he would give a ball for "P.L.U.," he set in motion a chain of anxiety and anticipation that spread across two continents. Inspired by Cecil Beaton's black-and-white confections in *My Fair Lady*'s famous Ascot scene, Capote's "Black and White Dance" of 1966 ultimately turned the spotlight on more than five hundred of society's creamiest. Among those who attended:

Billy Baldwin	Darryl Zanuck	Marella Agnelli
Lauren Bacall	Lee Radziwill	Horst
Jason Robards	Kenneth Jay Lane	Cecil Beaton
Count and Countess Rodolfo Crespi	Candice Bergen (19 years old)	Slim Keith
	Penelope Tree (16 years old)	Edward Albee
Babe Paley	Norman Norell	Mia Farrow
Walter Cronkite	Brooke Astor	Frank Sinatra
Mr. and Mrs. Leland Hayward	Tatiana and Alexander Liberman	George Plimpton
Jerome Robbins		Harper Lee
Garbo	Philip Johnson	Diana Vreeland

WE'VE GOT TO STOP MEETING LIKE THIS...

All you need are a handful of guests and some paper and pencils.
The first person begins by writing the name of a man in
the room or a famous man. The paper is folded to
conceal the name, and passed to the next person,
who writes down the name of a woman in the room or
famous woman. Again, the paper is folded down, and
passed on. (This is repeated after each entry.) Person #3
writes how the two would meet. Person #4 writes what "he" would
say. Person #5 writes what "she" would say. Then the composition is read aloud.

DINNER IN THE MOVIES

Dinner at Eight, 1933
Social mores in the 1930s: women in long gowns, men in tails,
champagne and merrymaking in spades.

The Lady Eve, 1941
Snakes and charmers abound when ophiologist Henry Fonda
fails to recognize the most cunning snake of them all—Barbara
Stanwyck at a gala dinner aboard a cruise ship.

The Thin Man, 1934
In which Nick Charles assembles a rogue's gallery of possible
suspects for Christmas dinner, and reveals the true murderer
of Clyde Wynant.

Guess Who's Coming to Dinner, 1967
Sidney Poitier is the dubious guest of honor, Spencer Tracy
discourses on love, and steak is shared by all. Welcome to a
changing America.

PARLOR GAMES

Six Characters

Charades

Guerrilla Scrabble

Hinkie-Pinkie

Dictionary

Wham

Get the Guest

My Dinner with André, 1981
One of the longest—and pithiest—dinner conversations ever
shown on the big screen.

The Discreet Charm of the Bourgeoisie, 1972
Folly and futility (just some of Luis Buñuel's surrealistic satirical
touches) mar the efforts of three couples as they try to have a
civilized dinner party.

Hannah and Her Sisters, 1986
Another quintessential Woody Allen culture clash—this time
Brooklyn meets Brahmin at Thanksgiving in Manhattan.

Alice B. Toklas welcomed spring by presenting guests with a bowl of fresh asparagus, enhanced only with whipped cream and salt.

DINING AT HEARST CASTLE, SAN SIMEON

"When dinner was announced, we would file into the long, high-ceilinged dining room, with its narrow refectory table that was almost the length of the room itself. . . . A massive sideboard held a marvelous collection of silver, all rubbed to shining perfection. . . . Tomato ketchup bottles, A-1 sauce, and glass containers of paper napkins . . . were placed at intervals down the length of the table and were the permanent and incongruous centerpiece of that noble board."

—Slim Keith

Andy Warhol and kohl-eyed Edie Sedgwick were such tireless partygoers that *Time* magazine reported they went to "more parties than a caterer."

Unlike his guests, who spent handfuls of money on their one-of-a-kind masks, Truman Capote got his mask at F.A.O. Schwarz. It cost 39 cents.

charades was so popular in the 1940s and 50s that it was known simply as "the game" · 85

WEEKEND PARTIES

"For one thing, it's important to have an idea what your guests want to do.
You have to take that into consideration. I also think it's great to have plans, but not to
the point of exhaustion. I like taking it easy. That's how I am in general, and I feel
the same way for my guests. My motto: Do what you please when you want. No obligation.
And that goes for me when I'm a guest—I prefer not to be asked to do a lot!"

FOR THE IDEAL GUEST ROOM...

A stack of classics
The Big Sleep, Raymond Chandler
Other Voices, Other Rooms, Truman Capote
To Kill a Mockingbird, Harper Lee

Fresh flowers

Pretty soaps

Scented candle (and matches)
for the bathroom—use an egg cup
to hold the matches

Portable CD player and CDs

Screened windows that
open and close easily

Bedside water glass and pitcher

If you and your guests share the same bathroom,
make light of it: embroider the towels
"His," "Hers," and "Yours"

Two Advil under the pillow with a note
"from the hangover fairy"

Emergency toothbrush and toothpaste

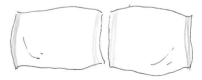

Fluffy pillows

Freshly laundered sheets, duvet, and towels

Bedside clock

Hangers

A good reading light

Magazines and books (magazines from the 1950s and 60s are fun, but magazines only a few years past their prime merely seem *old*)

Terrycloth robe and slippers. Embroider "Guest" on the robe and have several pairs of slippers embroidered with "Guest" on one foot and "Sleepy," "Best," and "Hungry" on the other.

"Down the stairs to the guest room—big bed—big cupboard—
lots of light—bowls of lovely soaps—boxes of candy—baskets
of fruit—the latest books—magazines—lovely sheets—
blankets—quilts—pillows—quiet—ring for breakfast."

—Katharine Hepburn, describing the guest room
at George Cukor's home in Los Angeles

TESTING THE WATER...

If you have houseguests frequently, it's a
good idea to sleep in your guest room once
every few months. Then you'll know firsthand
what works, what's missing, whether the
pillows are perfect or the mattress too soft.

FOR A PLEASANT SMELL,
TUCK LITTLE LAVENDER OR
MIXED-SPICE SACHETS AMONG
YOUR STORED BEDDING.

WEEKEND VIDEO FESTIVAL

The weekend is just about to begin. Go to your neighborhood
video store and stock up—although two or three films are the
most any of us actually watch.

Breakfast at Tiffany's/Guess Who's Coming to Dinner

Some Like It Hot/La Cage aux Folles

National Velvet/Babe

It Happened One Night/Two for the Road

Dial M for Murder/Les Diaboliques

Barefoot in the Park/Annie Hall

The Umbrellas of Cherbourg/Singin' in the Rain

Bonnie and Clyde/Jules et Jim

Rushmore/The Graduate

WEEKEND ACTIVITIES IN THE COUNTRY...

Second homes, late-night parties that last until dawn, or a visitor from out of town are all reasons for a weekend party. Do plan some activities in advance, but be sure to leave room for spontaneity.

Watch a tennis match

Pretend to relax

Fill your home library by going to an old book shop

Get up at dawn and go to the beach—take the newspaper, coffee, and a big blanket

Volunteer to weed the garden, sweep the porch, clean the pool

Read an old classic

Go canoeing at dusk

Build a fire

And remember, in the outdoors it's just you and the mosquitoes—protect yourself

Attend the firemen's pancake breakfast on Sunday

Put on stainproof clothes and go strawberry picking

SERVE RUBY RED GRAPEFRUIT WITH VIRGIN SEA BREEZES FOR BREAKFAST.

Gather wildflowers for the table

An Alphabet of Special Events

Anniversary Gifts · The After-Party Party
Barbecues · Birthdays · Brunches (and Lunches)
Farewell Dinners · Holidays · New Home
Picnics · Showers · Tailgate · Tea
Theme Parties · The Un-Occasion · Weddings

ANNIVERSARY GIFTS

"Of course Andy and I feel special about our actual wedding day. But the truth is that we've always celebrated three days—the day we started dating, the day we moved in together, and the day we married."

"The best anniversary gift I ever got was . . . Henry! He was my 10-year anniversary present from Andy."

1 PAPER *A Wonderful Time: An Intimate Portrait of the Good Life*, by Slim Aarons (1974)

2 COTTON Monogrammed kitchen towels: "You wash," "I'll dry"

3 LEATHER Leather laces for ice skates and a note indicating that a day at a special pond (near or far away), mugs of hot chocolate, and snow angels await

4 LINEN A turquoise linen-covered frame holding a favorite photo

5 WOOD New cedar shoe trees and ballroom dancing lessons

6 IRON An etch-a-sketch game and Saturday morning in bed watching cartoons and eating oatmeal

7 WOOL A wool stadium blanket (ivory with red, yellow, navy, and green stripes) and tickets to a football game (his) or outdoor theatrical performance (hers)

8 BRONZE A copy of *The Incredible Bronze Age Journey*, by James P. Grimes, and dinner at a neighborhood Greek restaurant (or better yet, a trip to Greece)

9 POTTERY Peruvian pottery coffee mugs, a pound of the best coffee you can get your hands on, and a new coffeemaker

10 TIN A copy of *The Wizard of Oz* and a red cashmere blanket because surely you *both* have a heart

15 CRYSTAL High tea beneath the crystal chandelier at the Pierre in New York

20 CHINA A pair of colorful decorative Chinese lamps

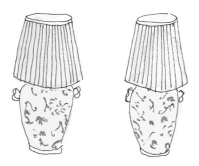

25 SILVER The U.S. military Silver Star is awarded for "gallantry in action." Have sterling silver cuff links or a sterling silver pendant made in the shape of a star engraved with your beloved's initials

30 PEARLS Have the words "pearls of wisdom" beautifully debossed on the cover of a photo album or journal. Fill the album with photos and memories or observations about the lessons you both have learned over the years

35 CORAL Go for dinner at the very best seafood restaurant in town and present your gift—a heavenly coral-colored cashmere sweater

40 RUBIES A bottle of lush, ruby red wine produced the same year you were married

45 SAPPHIRES A Schlumberger gold and blue paillonné enamel cuff bracelet and a night on the town celebrated with Bombay sapphire martinis

50 GOLD Gold anything—antique signet ring, Victorian sunburst mirror, Cuervo gold, a Glenn Miller collection of golden oldies, gold-rimmed champagne glasses

55 EMERALD A trip to the Tropics exploring exotic plants and birds, such as the Cuban emerald hummingbird

60 DIAMONDS Go to an evening baseball game and enjoy hotdogs and beer under the stars. Buy some popcorn and hide your gift in the box (something with a diamond), carefully tucked under the first layer of kernels

THE AFTER-PARTY PARTY

"I have to confess that sometimes I like the after-party as much as the party itself. I never think of the people who are still with us at the end of the evening as the hangers-on, but as the true soldiers of the night . . . and usually they're our closest friends. Suddenly, it's an after-party, Andy orders in pizza, and we all just happily slump. Talk about relaxed!"

BARBECUES

"Around our house barbecue usually means hamburgers and hot dogs, but there are so many farm stands where we live that sometimes we load up on armloads of fresh vegetables. When that happens, I call around to our friends and we put on a late-day grill of seasonal vegetables. Usually, I'll start with something simple like hummus and pita. And I'm a big believer in washing it down with really cold wine. One other thing: although I don't really want people to help out when we're throwing a party in the city, I'm more than happy for volunteers to cut up all the vegetables."

GRILLED SUMMER VEGETABLES

Begin with a variety of vegetables such as red peppers, eggplant, and zucchini. If you use portobello mushrooms, keep them whole, other-wise slice the vegetables in fairly generous shapes to make turning them easy—and so

they won't fall into the fire. Coat them with olive oil and kosher salt. Cook over a moderate heat, turning often. Delicious at room temperature. Garnish with fresh herbs.

BIRTHDAYS

"I must say that my husband, Andy, had a great 40th birthday celebration. We did a Mexican-themed party— even the little cocktail napkins and commemorative matches had 'Happy Birthday Andy' printed in Spanish. And we sang 'Happy Birthday' in Spanish too, though I can't say we were all that good. When we really just want to relax, Andy and I go to Mexico, which is where I've picked up a lot of brightly colored embroidered tablecloths and napkins, none of them expensive or fancy. We used the whole lot of them that night. (We also used a lot of 79¢ birthday candles from the grocery store—they're still the best.) Eleni gave Andy the cutest gift—forty of her amazing chicken-and-filo rolls. Andy adores these, so Eleni started him off with about ten, which she put in our freezer tied with a huge ribbon and card . . . he was completely surprised. Since then, she replenishes our stock from time to time."

BIRTHSTONES AND FLOWERS

JANUARY	Garnet	Carnation
FEBRUARY	Amethyst	Violet
MARCH	Aquamarine	Daffodil
APRIL	Diamond	Sweet Pea
MAY	Emerald	Lily-of-the-Valley
JUNE	Pearl	Rose
JULY	Ruby	Larkspur
AUGUST	Peridot	Gladiolus
SEPTEMBER	Sapphire	Aster
OCTOBER	Opal	Calendula
NOVEMBER	Topaz	Chrysanthemum
DECEMBER	Turquoise	Narcissus

BRUNCHES (AND LUNCHES)

"I can be just a bit lazy on a Sunday, and if we're in the city, brunch to me is not something we cook, but something we go to. And this works out perfectly when we have friends visiting. So for me, brunch begins with a little excursion, maybe a visit to the Guggenheim, and then perfect mimosas and Bloody Marys at the Carlyle, a place we adore. When I think of a place to go, the atmosphere and presentation matter as much as the food, especially if we're in the city. Then I like a super-urban setting with beautiful silverware and linens. If we're out at the beach, then my taste is dead opposite: I want simple simple simple. Absolutely nothing gimmicky. If we're traveling, I feel it's a perfect excuse for indulgence. So I let breakfast hours slide . . . until it's late enough to order brunch in our room. Now *that's* heaven."

FAREWELL DINNERS

"To start, a farewell dinner should be all about the guests of honor, so I would make sure that everything we serve is their favorite, beginning with the champagne (budget permitting!) and ending with the dessert. I'm a big believer that a dinner for a special occasion should have a little something that you can take home with you, so I might set mini menus before each plate with the

new address of our friends on the back side. As a farewell gift for departing friends, I'd get a beautiful address book and fill it with everyone's name and address. That way our friends would have a memento and something useful."

SEND-OFF SUPPER

Stuffed Artichokes

Grilled Angus Steak

Potatoes Anna

Sautéed Broccoli Rabe with Garlic and Lemon

Individual Gingerbread Soufflés

HOLIDAYS

Which came first? The holiday or the occasion? Holidays are when everything—and everyone—gets a little spruced up. The fun part is sharing the day or evening with your family or closest friends.

NEW YEAR'S DAY

"It's tempting to stay inside on New Year's Day, but after sleeping in, I love to bundle up and go for a walk in the park, especially if it's sunny and cold. First, however, I put a pot of New Year's Day chili on the stove to simmer. It's what Andy calls our "blinner"—breakfast, lunch, and dinner combined—and it's perfect after a night of drinking champagne. I wouldn't worry about

making the chili from scratch, either. If we don't have time, there's always a good restaurant or caterer whose chili we like to stock up on. And for us, chili isn't complete without saltine crackers."

VALENTINE'S DAY

"As nice as it is to spend the night with your special someone, it can be a total ball to be with a close circle of friends. For instance, throw a 'favorite couples' party, inviting friends to come as iconic duos— Hepburn and Tracy, Fred and Ginger, Bonnie and Clyde, Popeye and Olive Oyl. My friend Eleni makes the most amazing heart-shaped brownies, which she serves with raspberry sorbet, so I'd have these for dessert, along with a flute of Prosecco, garnished with a raspberry."

ST. PATRICK'S DAY

"My friends like to tease me about being Irish, so occasionally I cave in and invite close friends for a St. Patrick's Day dinner. Recently we did an all-green meal—chilled pea soup with a garnish of spring pea shoots, spinach pasta with walnut pesto sauce, and perfect mounds of green tea ice cream with thin, crispy pistachio biscotti. Crazy as it was, I did my

best not to go overboard with the theme—no green beer or kelly green cupcakes (although kelly green cupcakes could be funny, if they were served on beautiful china dessert plates and complemented by elegant glasses of port)."

EASTER

"We shared last Easter with our dear friend Pamela, and she created such a fun, simple touch for the dinner table. While her kids were making Easter eggs, she wrote each guest's name in wax on a hard-boiled egg, and then dipped them in Easter egg dye. She chose great colors—pink, green, yellow, and purple—and set them near the water glass at each place setting. The kids ate theirs, of course. I saved ours and put them in the egg tray in the refrigerator, just because. Andy and I don't do too much at our house, though Andy does like to hide a little basket filled with goodies."

MOTHER'S DAY

"Although this may not sound terribly inventive, I really do believe that flowers and a warm note make the perfect gift for mom. Don't send just any flowers, of course. Take the time to think about either a type of flower you know she loves (Did she mention hydrangea? Well then, send a dozen of these huge and amazing flowers), or her favorite color (She loves peach? Then ask the local florist to do an arrangement in shades of orange, peach, coral, and tangerine). I'd suggest finding the time to write a heartfelt note to send along with beautiful flowers rather than spending hours hunting for the ideal gift, although if you'd like to do both, I'm sure your mother would appreciate it!"

MEMORIAL DAY

"Memorial Day . . . the classic kickoff to the summer enter-taining season. I'd like to say that Andy and I go all out and host a Memorial Day barbecue, but the reality is we like to have friends over for dinner on Saturday night of the long weekend. (Let's be honest: this allows time to enjoy the weekend, rather than dashing around doing errands in anticipation of Monday afternoon.) I do keep the menu in the spirit of Memorial Day—classic burgers on the grill (wonderful with blue cheese tucked inside the burger), and bread-and-butter pickles and homemade ketchup on top."

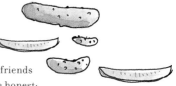

FATHER'S DAY

"Doesn't it seem like all dads like nuts? I've noticed that they're always a hit at cocktail parties (although I admit I never serve them), and it's rare that men don't go for them by the handful. For Father's Day, look for a great vintage wooden farmer's bowl or bucket and fill it with pistachios or peanuts in the shell."

FOURTH OF JULY

"On the Fourth, Andy and I always make sure we see a parade. We're lucky because the local parade goes right by our house on Long Island. It's one of those events that just feels like it's been going on forever. Which it probably has. The other thing we usually do is host an outdoor summer party. Rather than using basic hardware store coolers for all the beverages, last year Andy bought large blue and red tin tubs at Target. A friend who was staying with us for the weekend made a star stencil and painted a random pattern all over the outside of the tubs using white paint. We filled them with ice and used them to keep everything cold at our picnic."

LABOR DAY

"The only reason I duck out of hosting a barbecue for Labor Day is that our good friends Elyce and Andy have such a great Labor Day get-together every year. As the guest instead of the hostess, I always try to bring something that will make throwing the party easier for them. Barbecued chicken was on the menu last year, so I brought them a dozen flour sack towels (good for wiping greasy fingers), tied up with a colorful twill ribbon. Sounds like an ordinary gift, but it certainly was appreciated by guests and hosts alike. A bouquet of daisies spruced up my practical gift."

THANKSGIVING

"Thanksgiving dinner is one of the most beautiful, heartwarming occasions of the year. First and foremost, I value the time with family and friends. But then . . . the color! If you've mastered the turkey-stuffing-mashed potatoes-gravy routine, have fun with your table. Brown, pink, orange, and red are sumptuous colors and when they're combined . . . well, I can't imagine a more gorgeous setting. Combine pink napkins with brown and white decorative plates and your best sterling. If you can find red maple leaves at your local florist, use a silver metallic pen to write the names of your guests on the leaves and use them as name cards."

CHRISTMAS

"I adore the holiday season and one of my absolute favorite traditions is the classic Christmas tree. One of our most memorable trees was decorated with vintage bulbs — in blues, silvers, and whites — and all sorts of bird ornaments, from Mexican ceramic doves to antique German partridges. We had such fun hunting in flea markets and antique shops to find our crazy tree decorations."

NEW HOME

"The choices are endless, but one thing I wouldn't want to be accused of is adding any more clutter to someone's new home. I think an early act of kindness is to send someone breakfast and dinner for the first few days at their new place. Instead of having to root around for the coffee maker in the morning, it's so much nicer to get a delivery of fresh coffee and croissants. I'd still want to do something more lasting, so I'd probably give one of my favorite presents, big fluffy pillows, which I think everyone can always use, or else embroidered hand towels."

PICNICS

"A picnic always *sounds* fun, but then there are the bugs
and the heat and whether or not the ground is clean, so
what I like to do is more of a portable feast—something a
little more spruced up. I like to pack throws and cushions,
which are always comfortable and an indulgence if you
want to lie back and stare at the sky. I do think it's nice to
use pottery or china plates, so I wrap them in oversized
cloth napkins to keep them from breaking, and I find that
the napkins come in handy, too. Since I tend to stock up
on inexpensive farmers' market bags—they're so colorful
and big—we use these for hauling everything we need."

SHOWERS

"I pretty much like any reason for a party, and there is something
very dear about showers for brides and their new babies. For a baby
shower, I'd want all the food small: deviled eggs, cocktail-size hot
dogs, plates of little sugar cookies with pretty icing. For a bridal
shower, I'd fuss much more over the decorations—a white tablecloth
edged in a turquoise rick-rack and contrasting turquoise cotton napkins with white rick-rack ties,
brightly colored water glasses, and my best silver. All the flowers would be white and very fragrant,
such as peonies or tuberose, massed in small glass bowls down the length of the table."

TAILGATE

"When it comes to planning a tailgate today, I like to bring everything in
vintage rattan, which to me recalls those great old cars from the 1950s and
60s. A great rattan hamper, kitted out with bamboo-handled flatware, glasses
with rattan cup holders, and white restaurant ware—again, something from
the past such as Hall china—all suggest the warmth and tradition of a tailgate.
Depending on the weather, we might bring thermoses of Bloody Marys and
hot coffee. Another reason I like tailgates is that they offer the freedom of a
picnic but without the bugs."

TEA—THÈ—TÉ—CHA—CHAI

"In a way, a tea party is more of an indulgence than a cocktail party or super-elegant dinner for six, mainly because who has the time? But if I did— which I would dearly love to someday—then I'd go all out with the dishes and glasses and have flowers everywhere."

TEA IS THE MOST ELEGANT OF SMALL GATHERINGS AND IS THE HIGH-WATER MARK OF GRACIOUS SOCIALIZING...

Meet your mother at the city's finest hotel. Drink tea out of china cups and take dainty bites of several pastries.

Home brewed is best. Have high tea out on the patio in summer. Use your prettiest bone china and cloth napkins. Prepare an assortment of little sandwiches (cucumber and dill, chopped egg and caviar, goat cheese and mâche). Practice "pouring out" before the party.

Devote a year to sampling tea foods and condiments from around the world—madeleines, clotted cream, scones, wagashi, biscuits, crème fraîche, raspberry preserves, palmiers, lavender-lemon tea cakes.

For a lyrical note to your tea party, serve the verveine herbal tisane from Harney & Sons, based in Salisbury, Connecticut, the couturiers of the tea world. Or, invoke the corridors of India with Harney's chai tea—heat milk with water until heated through, stir in their chai blend, demerara sugar, and simmer 4 minutes. A spa for the senses.

A WORD ABOUT TEA: ITS HISTORY, CUSTOMS, PARAPHERNALIA, AND OTHER TRIVIA

Thanks to the hunger pangs of Anna, 7th Duchess of Bedford, AFTERNOON TEA came into fashion in the early 1800s. Like most of us, she was looking for a way to stem her appetite between lunch and dinner.

The ubiquitous TEA BAG dates back less than a hundred years, when a New York City merchant used a small piece of silk to hold tea leaves. Oddly, just as the Roaring Twenties came of age so did the tea bag, for the 1920s were also known as "the decade of the tea bag."

One of the finer specimens of tea paraphernalia is unquestionably the TEA CADDY, which the Europeans made out of silver, crystal, stoneware, and wood to store their precious tea leaves. Caddy spoons were no less beautifully designed. Of special note were those with a bowl fashioned like a scallop shell. (It seems that the Chinese used to pack their tea chests with a real scallop shell so that potential buyers could scoop a sample to sniff.) In addition to the scallop shell other traditional motifs are leaves, acorns, salmon, thistles, shovels, a jockey's cap, hand, and eagle wing.

Some purists believe that only DEMERARA SUGAR should be used to sweeten brewed tea. This raw sugar, with its coarsely textured uneven crystals, hails from the Demerara region of Guyana. As for adding dairy to tea, banish milk derivatives and go for the mother lode: whole milk or, better still, fresh cream.

Teas I adore from AROUND THE GLOBE . . . from China: gunpowder green, blooming green peony, spring rosettes; from Japan: first flush sencha, hojicha, gyokuro; from India: Darjeeling, Assam, Nilgiri; from Russia: Anastasia, Prince Vladimir, Russian Caravan; from England: Earl Grey, English Breakfast, Queen Anne, Royal Blend. And in the U.S., there is American Classic Tea, grown near Charleston, South Carolina, the official tea of the White House since 1987.

PEACH BASIL ICED TEA

3 tea bags—orange pekoe or any mild black tea
About 1 cup basil leaves
3 cups peach nectar, chilled
$\frac{1}{4}$ cup simple syrup
Peach slices and basil sprigs for garnish

Bring about a quart of water just to the boil, and pour over the tea and basil. Allow to steep 5 minutes, then strain into a heatproof pitcher. Cool tea, then chill, covered, about 1 hour or until cold. Stir in the peach nectar and syrup, to taste. Serve in tall clear glasses with the peach and basil garnishes. Makes 6 servings

For the simple syrup: Combine $1\frac{1}{4}$ cups water and $1\frac{1}{3}$ cups sugar in a saucepan. Bring to a boil, stirring, until the sugar is completely dissolved. Remove from heat and cool. (The syrup will keep for about 2 weeks.)

SUN TEA

6 tea bags, Constant Comment
Orange and lemon slices, strawberries, and fresh mint sprigs for garnish

In an attractive pitcher, combine the tea bags and 6 cups water. Set in a sunny spot to steep, about 4 hours. If desired, sweeten with simple syrup. Just before serving, float orange and lemon slices in the pitcher and stir in sliced strawberries. Serve in tall glasses over ice with fresh mint.

THEME PARTIES

Almost any event can become a "theme party"—it's all in the approach you take.

ACADEMY AWARDS NIGHT—Make score cards, take bets, and be sure to turn up the volume. What counts is not the acting, of course, but the costumes and the jewelry!

SUMMER SOLSTICE—Go to the roof, go to the nearest park, go out to your backyard, but be sure to swoop up a bunch of friends and toast the solstice with sea breezes. Designate someone to read aloud from Whitman's *Songs of Myself.*

TACKY EVERYTHING—"One year Andy's mother decided that since 'tacky' was getting a bad rap, she would celebrate it and give a tacky party. To start, all the food was pre-packaged, so there were small bags of corn chips and Cheez Doodles, vacuum-sealed packets of chipped beef and ham, deli-size packets of mayonnaise, ketchup, and mustard, individually wrapped slices of American cheese, Hostess cupcakes and Twinkies, and lots of candy bars. She used plastic for all the plates, cups, and forks, and for serving pieces she used containers like Tupperware. It was a hoot."

MONTHLY FILM GROUP—Watch *Love Story* and make it an all-American evening complete with college food, such as macaroni and cheese, pork chops, and Rolling Rock beer. Don't forget potato chips and a box of Kleenex.

FOR THE LOVE OF
CHOCOLATE—Forget about
cholesterol and indulge. Invite
friends over for dessert and
make it an international ode to
the cacao bean: hot chocolate
soufflé, tiramisu, Hostess
cupcakes, pain au chocolat, chocolate licorice, chocolate-covered strawberries, chocolate Necco
wafers, chocolate-covered malt balls, chocolate mousse, double chocolate ice cream. Serve
everything on pink plates, set out bowls of perfectly mounded whipped cream, and be prepared
to do some heavy laundering of your white napkins the next day.

SLIDE SHOW OF YOUR TRIP TO THE HERMITAGE MUSEUM IN ST. PETERSBURG—
Be prepared to woo your guests with vodka shots and blintzes heaped with caviar.
They'll be good for at least two carousels of slides.

CHINESE NEW YEAR—Ask everyone to wear red, which
will assure them a bright future. Set out place cards or
menus in red. As party favors, give each person a Chinese
lunar calendar with the 12 signs of the zodiac (represented
by the rat, ox, tiger, rabbit, dragon, snake, horse, sheep,
monkey, rooster, dog, and boar). Custom order fortune
cookies, with descriptions of
your favorite books, movies,
or shops, and give them to
your friends.

THE UN-OCCASION

"Over the years, we've had countless gatherings with friends that began as 'Come by for a drink' and wound up being a full-fledged all-evening affair. Pretty much any event can become an un-occasion, but this kind of party works best for those spontaneous moments when the urge (and idea) strikes. When Andy was in Little League, his mother threw him what became his first un-occasion party: to celebrate his first hit at bat (never mind that he fouled out). She invited the team over, rushed home from the game, and served sandwiches, cream soda, and Twinkies."

BEING PREPARED FOR THE UN-OCCASION...

"If you see cocktail napkins you love—cloth or linen— purchase them for future use. Solid colors are fun. Themed napkins are also adorable. My favorite is a set beautifully embroidered with wild animals."

"Stash hors d'oeuvres picks and swizzle sticks in a designated 'party accessory' drawer. These will come in handy if friends stop by for cocktails before going out for dinner."

"Keep a mix of music in your collection. If you have a friend or two over to catch up and decide to order in Mexican food, it'll be more fun to have salsa music playing in the background."

"Know your local restaurants. Having faith in your neighborhood haunts means that you can place an order at 6:30 and know it will arrive at your requested time of 8:00 P.M. Now this is what I mean by spontaneous entertaining!"

"Flowers are essential. Even if you have to pick them up at the local grocery store, take the time to put a loose bunch in a vase and snip a bud to put in the bathroom—I think this is always a nice touch."

"When staying in beats going out—one evening Eleni and Randall stopped by and we realized we were too bushed to go out, so we ordered in pizza. That part was basic. But then we did a little window dressing—we cut the pie into little squares and speared each one with a colored toothpick. I used some country napkins, Andy opened a chianti, and it was 'hello home, so long restaurant!'"

WEDDINGS

"Considering that I'm such a traditionalist in so many ways, I'm completely unconventional in my thinking about weddings—or at least I was about mine. To this day, I don't wear a diamond ring or wedding band (though I do love wearing vintage cocktail rings). So if I had any advice to give, it would be that you should have the wedding that makes you happy and comfortable. It takes a lot of work just finding the right person, so go easy on yourself when it comes to the wedding itself."

"Even though Kate is casual about most wedding traditions, naturally she wanted the day we got married to be special. The flowers were great, the music was just right, and Kate's dress was amazing. Kate has a thing about candles, especially votives, so she had them strategically placed around the house, even along the staircase. Kate made her arrival coming down the stairs, but there was one problem—the votives caught on the train of her wedding dress and set it on fire. To her credit, Kate burst out laughing, and whatever notions either of us had about the day being 'precious' went out the window, so to speak."

—Andy Spade

THANK YOU

It seems that every project I venture upon involves the helping hands of many people, and this book is no exception. Everyone has pitched in—from my husband and colleagues at *kate spade* to my dog, Henry, indispensable bon vivant and critic.

Julia Leach, who oversees our creative department and is a longtime friend of Andy's and mine, has truly shouldered the responsibility of putting this book together. I don't know how she manages to have so much energy and such grace under pressure, but she is a godsend. Working in tandem with Julia is our editor and new friend, Ruth Peltason, whose enthusiasm and expertise have helped all of us make this book special. They were joined in their efforts by Virginia Johnson, our gifted illustrator; designer Alberta Testanero, whose whimsical flair and talent are evident on every page; and Ana Rogers, who took over the design and shepherded the book to completion.

Our business partners, Elyce Arons and Pamela Bell, and I were friends long before we started this company, and they have been greatly supportive of this project. Their suggestions, their own experiences, and memories of parties we've gone to together have all contributed to *Occasions*. So has the friendship and encouragement extended by Robin Marino, president of *kate spade*. I'm grateful to Marybeth Schmitt, who has skillfully navigated our publicity efforts. Also at our office I would like to thank Susan Anthony, Barbara Kolsun, Stacy Van Praagh, Meg Touborg, and everyone in our creative department—Biz Zast, Lawren Howell, Jenifer Ruske,

Cheree Berry, Naseem Niaraki, and Anthony Coombs. Katie Powell Brickman cheerfully provided research.

Over the years my close friend Eleni Gianopulos continually adds fun to every occasion, and makes even something simple memorable. When it comes to a party, Eleni's cookies and hors d'oeuvres are "required eating," and I can't imagine doing a book about festive times without her contributions. I also want to thank Peter Callahan, who has catered many parties for us with creativity and perfect pitch.

The business of publishing a book is new to me, and I am grateful that our agent, Ira Silverberg, has been so wonderfully wise. I have been fortunate to work with the devoted crew at Simon & Schuster, including David Rosenthal, executive vice president and publisher, whose enthusiasm wowed us all; Amanda Murray, our patient in-house editor; Walter L. Weintz; Michael Selleck; Tracey Guest; and Peter McCulloch. Thank you, thank you.

And then there's my husband, Andy, who first gave me the courage to go into business more than a decade ago and now into books. "We already have so many books and we both love to read," I told him, "do you really think it's a good idea to try being an author?" Well, his answer is before you. Andy's ideas and his infectious spirit and voice are in *Occasions*, page for page. So, too, is his encouragement, his humor, and his love. I am indeed blessed.

Kate Spade

SELECT BIBLIOGRAPHY

Bourdon, David. *Warhol.* New York: Harry N. Abrams, Inc., 1989.

Dariaux, Geneviève Antoine. *Entertaining with Elegance: A Complete Guide for Every Woman Who Wants to Be the Perfect Hostess On All Occasions.* Garden City, N.Y.: Doubleday and Company, Inc., 1965.

Editors of *Esquire* Magazine and Scotty and Ronnie Welch. *Esquire Party Book.* Illustrations by Seymour Chwast. New York: Esquire Inc., in association with Harper and Row, 1935. Reprint ed. 1965.

Ferguson, Claire. *Picnics and Portable Feasts.* San Diego, Calif.: Laurel Glen Publishing, 2001.

Gallagher, Nora. *Parlor Games.* Reading, Mass.: Addison-Wesley Publishing Co., 1979.

Gunn, Lilian M. *Table Service and Decoration.* Philadelphia: J. B. Lippincott Co., 1935.

Hepburn, Katharine. *Me: Stories of My Life.* New York: Alfred A. Knopf, 1991.

Keith, Slim, with Annette Tapert. *Slim: Memories of a Rich and Imperfect Life.* New York: Simon & Schuster, 1990.

Krauss, Ruth. *Open House for Butterflies.* Illustrations by Maurice Sendak. New York: Harper and Row Publishers, 1960.

MacDougall, Alice Foote. *Coffee and Waffles.* Garden City, N.Y.: Doubleday, Page and Co., 1926.

Mendelson, Cheryl. *Home Comforts: The Art and Science of Keeping House.* New York: Scribner, 1999.

Post, Emily. *Etiquette: The Blue Book of Social Usage.* New York: Funk & Wagnalls Co., Publishers, 1945. Reprint 1949.

———. *The Personality of a House: The Blue Book of Home Charm.* New York: Funk & Wagnalls, 1939.

Root, Waverley. *Food: An Authoritative and Visual History and Dictionary of the Foods of the World.* New York: Simon & Schuster, 1980.

Scott, Joseph, and Donald Bain. *The World's Best Bartenders' Guide.* New York: Berkley Publishing Group and HP Books, 1998.

Vanderbilt, Amy. *Amy Vanderbilt's New Complete Book of Etiquette: The Guide to Gracious Living.* Garden City, N.Y.: Doubleday and Co., Inc., Reprint, 1967.

White, Katharine S. *Onward and Upward in the Garden.* Edited and with an introduction by E. B. White. New York: Farrar, Straus, Giroux, 1979.

Young, Carolin C. *Apples of Gold in Settings of Silver.* New York: Simon & Schuster, 2002.

LOST HORS D'OEUVRES

Petals 'n Pickles, Hawaiian Meatballs, Kleiner Liptauer,
Hot Crab Dunk, Cheese Pennies, Swedish Meatballs, Rumaki,
Nippy Carrot Nibbles, Gouda Burst, Cossack's Delight,
Oyster in the Patty Shell, Rye Ribbon Round, Sunburst
Deviled Eggs, Harlequin Dip, Sausage Frills, Cheese Dainties,
Fish Quickies, Six-in-One Cocktail Hash, Confetti
Chicken Spread, Redheaded Pâté, Dipsidoodle Crab Dip.

SKRUMPIES

Rinse and core 1 pint cherry tomatoes. Combine a 7 ½-ounce can crab meat,
½ cup mayonnaise, 2 teaspoons scallions, and a dash of Worcestershire.
Stuff the tomatoes with the crab mixture. Serves 8

Editors: Ruth A. Peltason, for Bespoke Books
             Julia Leach, for kate spade

Art Director: Alberta Testanero
Designer: Ana Rogers

The author and publisher gratefully acknowledge
those writers whose works contributed to this book.

SIMON & SCHUSTER
Rockefeller Center
1230 Avenue of the Americas
New York, NY 10020

For information regarding special discounts for bulk purchases, please contact
Simon & Schuster Special Sales at 1-800-456-6798 or business@simonandschuster.com

Manufactured in Italy

10 9 8 7 6 5 4 3 2 1

Library of Congress Cataloging-in-Publication Data

Spade, Kate.
    Occasions : always gracious, sometimes irreverent / by Kate Spade ; edited by Ruth
Peltason and Julia Leach ; illustrations by Virginia Johnson.
        p. cm.
    Includes bibliographical references.
    1. Entertaining. 2. Cookery. I. Peltason, Ruth A. II. Leach, Julia (Julia E.) III. Title.
TX731.S675 2004
642'.4–dc22
                                                                          2003062971
ISBN 0-7432-5065-6